A

for All

Published by
Lotus Press

Ayurveda for All

Dr. Rajeev Sharma
B.H.M.S.; M.D; P.G.N.D; D.Y.Th;PMS

4263/3, Ansari Road,
Darya Ganj, New Delhi-110002

LOTUS PRESS
4263/3, Ansari Road, Darya Ganj,
New Delhi-110002 • Ph.: 32903912, 23280047
E-mail: lotus_press@sify.com • www.lotuspress.co.in

AYURVEDA FOR ALL
© 2011 Lotus Press
ISBN: 978-81-8382-254-1

All rights reserved. No part of this publication may be reproduced, stored in a retrieval system, or transmitted, in any form or by any means, mechanical, photocopying, recording or otherwise, without prior written permission of the publisher.

Please consult your physician before trying any medicine or treatment plan. Author/Publisher will not be responsible for any reaction/loss.

Published by: Lotus Press, New Delhi
Printed at: Anand Sons, Delhi

Preface

Ayurveda is an ancient science of Indian origin. It was the long research of our Rishis which took place in the sape of Ayurveda.

The School of Physicians (Atreya) and the School of Surgeons (Dhanvantari) epitomized the eight main areas of ayurvedic studies and specialization during ancient times. The details of these eight branches of this natural alternative medicine are present in the three ancient ayurvedic texts of: Charaka Samhita, Susruta Samhita and Astanga Hridaya.

Besides Charak and Sushrut Samhita, Bhaishajya Bhaskar, Vanoshadhi Chandrodya etc. are some of our ancient and accepted Ayurvedic Text Books.

In this book I have given a short history and philosophy of Ayurveda alongwith doshas and theory and elements. There is a big role of food in Ayurveda, which I have discussed separately alongwith Panchkarma and role of spices.

Five element theory and vatta, pitta, kapha characteristics are discussed well. There is a separate chapter on Rasayan Chikitsa, which play an important role in Ayurveda.

Disorders from mind and head to toe too are discussed chapter wise. Thus, this is a Family Ayurvedic Guide. So why it is named "Ayurveda for All".

If anybody wants to come and consult me, first fix an appointment by phone or email and please do not come without prior appointment.

With thanks and regards,

Dr. Rajeev Sharma
E-mail: drs108@gmail.com

A Brief About Dr. Rajeev Sharma

Dr. Rajeev Sharma is an eminent consultant of Homoeopathy, Yoga, Naturopathy and Alternative Medicine in India. He has written more than two hundred and fifty books (250) in Hindi and English and around one thousand articles which have been published in various newspapers and magazines. He was also an Editional Board Member of the prestigious *Asian Homoeopathic Journal* besides many other newspapers and magazines.

Dr. Rajeev Sharma has written books on ayurveda, allopathy, homoeopathy, yoga, naturopathy, accupressure, magnetotherapy, reiki, water-therapy, massage and aromatherapy etc.

The books written by Dr. Rajeev Sharma are published by renowned publishers of India. Besides this he is doing editing and translation also. He is content provider to many magazines.

Dr. Rajeev Sharma has written books on all major ailments like diabetes, hypertension, obesity, stomach and respiratory disorders, E.N.T. disorders, female disorders, UTI disorders, paediatric problems, headache, stress and other mental problems and Sexual Disorders etc. You can fix an appointment for any of such problem.

Dr. Rajeev Sharma is Medical Advisor to Ralson Remedies (a homoeopathic manufacturer), and Dixit Pharmacy (Ayurvedic Manufacturer), and Medical Officer in U.P. Govt.

He has received several prizes for his outstanding achievements. He has been awarded the *Best Author prize in Hindi* by the Ministry of Health and Family Welfare,

Government of India and *Sarjana Puraskar by U.P. Hindi Sansthan*, Lucknow. He has delivered talks on All India Radio and lectures on Alternative Medicine in various Government and Non-government Organisations. He has written Advt. Scripts for the products of several companies.

He is delivering lectures and providing literature on Yoga, Pranayama, Meditation, Stress and Life Style Management to the MNC's and corporate houses.

He has established a website through which you can get Online Training or e Books in Accupressure, Massage, Yoga, Water Therapy, Diet Therapy, Naturopathy, Colour Therapy and Reiki besides other paramedical courses.

Dr. Rajeev Sharma is also a social activist. He has worked a lot against Addiction and prevention of AIDS.

He has worked for human rights too and has received the World Human Rights Promotion Award. His name has been published in *LIMCA BOOK OF RECORDS* and is to be published in India Book of Records 2011.

He has developed a website :- **www.newkamasutra.com** : A site of love, romance and sex.

Newkamasutra is a scientific site to guide for love, romance, relationship, dating, sex related and other problems. The information given here is not porn but scientific, relevant and authentic. You can update your knowledge by viewing "Vatsyayan's Kamasutra", "Newkamasutra", "Dating and Romance", "Sex Education", "Sexual Disorders", "Aphrodisiacs and Diets", "Sex Yoga" etc pages.

Besides this you can do "Consultation" and "Online Courses" or purchase an "eBook" of your choice or shop from "Store". "Forum" also provide facility to interact with viewers of our site.

We do not believe in magical remedies or untrue claims. We treat individuals on the basis of the totality of their symptoms. Thus the consultation and medicines provided are personalized. The ultimate aim of our organization is to provide quality information, medicines, teachings and techniques. This is called **QMT**.

Contents

i	Preface	(v)
ii	A Brief About Dr. Rajeev Sharma	(vii)

Part I

1.	Ayurvedic History and Philosophy	13
2.	Ayurvedic Studies—Introduction	17
3.	Rasayan Chikitsa	23
4.	Characteristics of Vata, Pitta, Kapha	30
5.	Stages of Disease	35

Part II

6.	Methods of Preparation of Ayurvedic Medicines	38
7.	Concepts of Mental Health in Ayurveda	40
8.	Disorders of Eyes, Ears and Nose	49
9.	Disorders of Throat, Mouth and Teeth	62
10.	Disorders of Respiratory System	69
11.	Disorders of Digestive System	76
12.	Disorders of Muscles and Joints	96
13.	Skin and Hair Problems	104
14.	Disorders of Kidney & Urinary System	119
15.	Disorders of Females	122
16.	Disorders of Male and Aphrodisiacs (Bajikaran)	131
17.	High Blood Pressure & Other Heart Problems	137
18.	Different Fevers	145

Part III

19.	Different Tastes	152
20.	Role of Food in Balancing the Doshas	156

21.	Reducing Imbalance by Diets	159
22.	Food According to Property	166
23.	Food Combining	171

Part IV

24.	Wheat Grass	174
25.	Medicinal Properties of Barley / Maize / Rice / Wheat	183
26.	Medicinal Properties of Honey / Milk / Sugarcane /Curd	187
27.	Juices for Healthy Life	192
28.	Magic of Water	198
29.	Medicinal Properties of Pulses / Seeds / Nuts	200
30.	General & Medicinal Properties of Fruits	211
31.	Use of Vegetables to Cure Different Diseases	216
32.	Condiments and Spices as Medicines	234

Part V

33.	Panchakarma and Other Ayurvedic Treatments	240
34.	Five Element Theoy Air, Earth, Water, Fire, Ether	248

Part VI

35.	Drugs and Herbs of Ayurveda used in Treatment of Cancer	255

Part – I

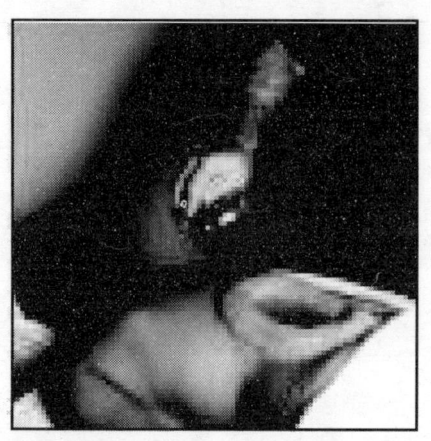

1

Ayurvedic History and Philosophy

As knowledge of Ayurveda spread to other civilizations, its adaptability was recognized and it was often integrated into local forms of medicine. Ayurveda had a profound effect on the medicine of Tibet, China, Persia, Egypt, Greece, Rome, and Indonesia.

HISTORY

Ayurveda was discovered and developed by ancient Indian holy men known as "Rishis." Due to their relationship (connectedness) to both the spiritual and physical worlds, they were able to discern the basic nature of the universe and man's place in it. They developed an oral tradition of knowledge that was fluid and allowed for growth. As new therapies and herbs were discovered and trade brought new information from other cultures, Ayurveda was built. The Rishis were scientists who made huge advances in the fields of surgery, herbal medicine, the medicinal effects of minerals and metals, exercise, physiology, human anatomy, and psychology. Their surgeries included difficult procedures such as Caesarean section (successfully performed in the West only in the last 100 years). Passed down from teacher to student for centuries, this information was recorded when written language was developed: the Rig Veda (4500 years ago), the Atharva Veda, (3200 years ago) and others.

Ayurvedic medicine was suppressed in Indian during British colonial rule. In 1833, the East India Company closed and banned all Ayurvedic colleges. For almost 100 years, Ayurveda was known as "the poor man's medicine," practiced only in rural areas where western medicine was too expensive or unavailable.

With India's independence, Ayurveda has re-emerged to gain equal footing with "Western Medicine. In 1978, at a conference on Third World Medicine sponsored by the World Health Organization (WHO) of the United Nations, it was concluded that Ayurveda would be the best system of medicine for undeveloped countries. There is hope that a global medicine will be created with armaceutical products, are all favourable aspects for the world's population. Western, Chinese and traditional native medicines may be appropriately blended in each locale.

Philosophy

Ayurvedic theory believes that health results from harmony within one's self. To be healthy, harmony must exist between your purpose for being, your thoughts, your feelings, and your physical actions. Your purpose is peaceful, yet if your thoughts are fearful and your emotions negative, your physical body will manifest some disease as a "wake up call to change." In Ayurveda, the manifestation of disease is actually considered to be a good sign, because it reveals a previously hidden aspect of oneself...an aspect to be healed. Health is harmony within all aspects of self. This inner harmony also becomes manifest as harmony with family, friends, co-workers, society, and nature.

Often the first question an Ayurvedic physician may ask is: "What is your purpose in life? And what is its appropriate form (work, job, activity, etc.)? How are your relationships?" When harmony exists in these areas, physical healing is so much easier.

The goal of Ayurveda is true freedom from death and disease, enjoyment of uninterrupted physical, mental, and spiritual happiness and fulfilment. It may sound surprising, but according to Ayurvedic philosophy, enjoyment is one of life's purposes. But you can lose your ability to enjoy if you overindulge. Either you limit yourself or mother nature will limit you. We have more degenerative disease in the West because of our abundance and tendency to overindulge.

Ayurveda's Four Goals in Life

1. The fulfilment of your duties to society.
2. The accumulation of possessions while fulfilling duties.
3. Satisfying legitimate desires with the assistance of one's possessions.
4. The realization that there is more to life than duties, possessions and desires.

Ayurvedic philosophy believes that only a person with a strong immune system can be healthy. The practitioners identify the immune system as a fragment of nature (the Divine Mother). This gift from her creates us, sustains us, nourishes us, and protects us from outside invasion. As long as our immune system is strong, we suffer no disease. The ancient vedic word for immunity means "forgiveness of disease"- from the concept that negative thoughts and lifestyles cause disease. Disease, therefore, is a message about a need for change... if only we can understand this. In this sense, strength comes from transforming our projections about our symptoms. Healing comes from seeing adversity as a challenge, by taking back our negative thoughts about people and events. We can transform disease into a "perfect opportunity." Spiritual health, then, is a dynamic balance between a strongly integrated individual personality and nature (a nature that's understood to encompass all aspects of existence). This is only possible when people remember their debt to nature.

In summary: Ayurveda believes that health results from the relationship (the connectedness) between self, personality, and everything that goes into our mental, emotional, psychic, and spiritual being. It believes that health also results from good relations with others, from an acknowledged indebtedness to mother nature, from the realization of one's purpose, and from the pursuit of legitimate goals in life. Ayurvedic philosophy maintains the importance of a strong immune system, that forgiveness is strengthening and that immortality is possible.

•••

2

Ayurvedic Studies— Introduction

All ayurvedic studies conducted on herbal and holistic medicine in ancient time of India, followed from the fountainhead of the two principle ayurvedic schools. The School of Physicians (Atreya) and the School of Surgeons (Dhanvantari) epitomized the eight main areas of ayurvedic studies and specialization during ancient times. The details of these eight branches of this natural alternative medicine are present in the three ancient ayurvedic texts of: Charaka Samhita, Susruta Samhita and Astanga Hridaya.

Kayachikitsa, Internal Medicine

The word 'kaya' (body) not only refers to the gross body of a person but to the subtle body as well. This natural alternative medicine recognizes that the body of a person is the product of the constant psychosomatic interactions. The imbalances in the three doshas of vata-pitta-kapha occur sometimes by the mind and sometimes by the body's dhatu (tissues) and mala (toxin deposits). Hence, the kayachikitsa branch of this system of herbal and holistic medicine, delves deep into ascertaining the root cause of the illness. Then only a suitable treatment is recommended to bring back mind and body into balance. Though the prescription might give an impression that the treatment is meant for the physical body, these in fact have a strong impact on mind and soul of a person.

The Charaka Samhita is the most important scripture on kayachikitsa. It discussed the basic principles of treatment (mentioned above), various types of therapies and purification or detoxification methods i.e. panchakarma. But, its thrust area has been diagnosis of a disease. Detail account of various methods of diagnosis, study of various stages of symptoms and the comprehensive management of debilitating diseases like diabetes mellitus, tuberculosis, asthma and arthritic conditions.

The section of Nidana Sthana of Charaka Samhita deals with etiology, pathogenesis and diagnosis of an illness. Six stages of the development of disease are enumerated as aggravation, accumulation, overflow, relocation, build up in a new site and manifestation into a recognizable disease (it is interesting to note that modern medical science can only detect a disease during the fifth or sixth stages of the illness). In kayachikitsa there is always an opportunity to stop the disease at each stage preventing its full manifestation.

One of the significant methods of treatment under kayachikitsa is panchakarma. This is a method of reversing the disease path from its manifestation stage back into to its site of original development through special forms of emesis, purgation and enema etc. Another unique aspect of kayachikitsa is rejuvenation called kaya kalpa. The term kaya kalpa means renewal of body. According to ayurveda the human body is made of seven types of dhatu or tissues-structures—plasma, blood, muscle, fat, bone, marrow and reproductive fluids. To prolong the youthfulness of the body kayachikitsa applies several physical and mental disciplinary methods with special medicinal preparations, to rebuild the body's cells and tissues after the initial process of detoxification, through panchakarma.

SHALYA TANTRA, SURGERY

Contrary to the modern concepts surgery was pioneered by ayurveda in ancient India. It is a significant branch of ayurveda.

The name of the sage-physician Susruta is synonymous with surgery. From his treatise Susruta Samhita we come to know that thousand of years ago sophisticated methods of surgery were practiced in India.

The original text of Susruta discusses in detail about an exhaustive range of surgical methods including about how to deal with various types of tumours, internal and external injuries, fracture of bones, complications during pregnancy and delivery, and obstruction in intestinal loop. Susruta was the first surgeon to develop cosmetic surgery. His surgical treatment for trichiasis can be to some of the modern operative techniques used for this eye disease.

The use of various surgical instruments is also described in the Susruta Samhita for the treatment. The instruments described were made from stone, wood and other such natural materials.

Shalya Tantra was popular because this could give fast relief as compared to the slow process of recovery from medicines or herbs. Charaka the best-known physician of ayurvedic medicine also recommended for Shalya Tantra in treatment of certain diseases, which required immediate attention like hemorrhoids. The long foreign rule in India and lack of promotion stalled the progress of ayurvedic surgery in the middle of the second millennium.

Shalakya Tantra, opthalmology

This branch of ayurveda deals in details with the etiology, diagnosis, prognosis, prevention and treatment of diseases of head, ear, nose, eye and throat. The name of this branch was called Shalakya due to excessive use of 'Shalaka', which means a rod or probe. Though all the three main classics of ayurveda deals on this subject, Susruta Samhita describes more deeply about this branch. So much so that some of the classifications found in the Susruta Samhita are not even traced by the modern medical science. It described five types of pterygium, and the prognosis it made about aveitis and glaucoma has not been improved since. In fact he is the first surgeon in medical history who systematically and elaborately dealt with anatomical structure of eye.

Susruta has discussed about 72 diseases of the eye. He has stipulated drug therapy for various types of conjunctivitis and glaucoma along with surgical procedures of the removal of cataract, pterygium, diseases of ear, nose and throat besides cosmetic surgery for traumatized nose and ear (rhinoplasty and auraplasty). Apart from these complicated methods of treatment the three samhitas—Charaka, Susruta and Astanga Hridaya, recommended simple home remedies for minor problems like dryness of eye, migraine and mouth ulcers etc. which are being successfully administered even today.

AGADA TANTRA, TOXICOLOGY

Agada tantra or Toxicology branch of ayurveda described about various methods of cleaning the poisons out of the body as well as recommends antidotes for particular poisons. It deals with a wide range of natural toxins originating from wild lives (animals, birds, insects etc.), plants/herbs (belladonna, aconite etc.), vegetables, minerals (leads, mercury, arsenal etc.) and artificial poisons prepared from poisonous drugs. This branch also deals with air and water pollution, which are basically the causes of various dangerous epidemics.

The three samhitas described about this branch of toxicology, which also include description, and disadvantages of food of opposite qualities, drugs and food causing chronic poisoning symptoms. In ayurveda certain poisons are used as medicines after proper processing and quantification. Precious stones like diamond, ruby and poisonous minerals like lead and mercury were in use for this purpose. This branch also has information regarding fatal doses of various poisons, which are resorted to in a view to administer those into an enemy's body system.

KAUMARABHRITYA, PEDIATRICS

This branch of kaumarabhritya deals comprehensively about prenatal, postnatal baby care and gyneacology. With the view to achieve its ultimate aim of creating a healthy and disease free society ayurveda strives to make the baby from the time of its conception upto the time of its growth into an adult.

Kaumarabhritya has recognized that the mental and physical state of the mother has direct links with the health of the child. It has recommended particular diet, regimen, nutrition and conduct for women during and after delivery. So advanced was this science that thousands of years back Charaka described the growth and progress of fetus in minute detail. Even it mentioned about a technique called punsanvan vidhi for having a child of one's desired gender, intelligence and constitution. This branch meticulously dealt with the problem of infertility—its causes and treatment methods.

Apart from that kaumarbhritya deals with various disorders concerning children's health such as gastrointestinal diseases, teething disorder, rickets other than midwifery.

VAJIKARANA, SCIENCE OF APHRODISIACS

Ayurveda in this branch of science explains the art of producing healthy progeny for the creation of a better society. Hence, deals with various diseases like infertility and conditions relating to weak shukra dhatu or the vital reproductive fluids of the body. Apart from prescribing a lot of effective formulations to provide nutrition to enhance the quality of this vital body fluids it specifically emphasized to lead a highly disciplined life.

This branch of ayurveda highlighted that celibacy is essential for good health. It helps increase the will power, intellect and memory in addition to a healthy body. The shukra dhatu has a direct link with ojas or the immunity of the body. Hence, vajikaran prescribed the therapeutic use of various aphrodisiacs and tonic preparations for enhancing the vigour and reproductive capabilities of men that also strengthens other body tissues (dhatus) like muscles, fats, bones and blood.

Bhuta Vidya, psychiatry

This branch of ayurveda specifically deals with the diseases of mind or psychic conditions, which can be caused by super natural forces. Different experts have explained the word bhuta differently. Some experts say that bhuta means ghosts and similar bad spirits who cause abnormal psychological conditions. Others say bhuta represents microscopic organisms such as virus, bacteria that are not visible to naked eye. Ayurveda also believes in the past karma as a causative factor of certain diseases. Bhuta Vidya deals with the causes, which are directly not visible and have no direct explanation in terms of tridosha.

In many cases illness is caused by the disturbance of mind, where rajas (passion) and tamas (ignorance) are supposed to be the contributing factors. These problems can be related to modern psychiatry. Bhuta Vidya mention use of various disinfectant plants under the title of 'graha vidya dravya' for fumigation to make the atmosphere germ free. In addition to this herbs, diet, use of mantras and yogic therapies like meditation and pranayama to pacify the psychological disturbances of a patient.

• • •

3

Rasayan Chikitsa

Rasayana is a special type of treatment containing various methods of rejuvenation. It derives from 'Rasa' and 'Ayana.' The literal meaning of Rasa is the essence of something. Anything ingested into the body in the form of food or medicine is first resynthesized into Rasa Dhatu, the basic plasma tissue. Ayana is the method by which Rasa is carried to all the body tissues for biochemical metamorphosis (Rasakriya). The concept of Rasayana is based on these two principles of conservation and transmutation of energy. Rasayana therapy strives to improve physical, mental and moral qualities. It prevents old age, restores youthfulness, improves the complexion and the voice, increases physical strength and immunity. It strengthens memory and intelligence, gives happiness to oneself, and a life which is beneficial to others.

How the Rasayanas Help?

1. They slow down aging process.
2. They improve memory; increase concentration power, and curb agitation & anxiety.
3. Amalaki Rasayana is an amazing remedy for cold and cough. Also sweetens the voice and also clears hoarseness.
4. There are Rasayanas for dealing with mental disorders like hypertension, nervous debility, and memory disturbances etc.

5. They nourish lymph, blood, semen and adipose tissue.
6. They regenerate dead tissues and cells.
7. They prevent illness and degenerative changes, and therefore can free you from arthritis, senile diseases etc. You can consult an Ayurvedic specialist and take the Rasayanas according to your needs. However, remember that intake of these solutions involves some strict rules. You must stick to those for getting the best results.

RASAYANA WITH SPECIFIC PURPOSE:
- For improving longevity
- For improving brain function
- For improving action of the tissues
- For improving action of the channel systems
- For improving action of the senses

THE REJUVENATIVE PROGRAMS OF AYURVEDA

Rhythmic massages that relax each tendon. Medicated baths revitalize every nerve. Diets that restore you to sound health. The rejuvenation programs of Ayurveda are designed to improve your vitality, enhance immunity and increase longevity. Besides, good health goes a long way in bringing out the best in you. Adding a healthy glow to your skin, it will awaken the sleeping beauty within. Adding years to life, and life to your years.

REJUVENATION THERAPY (RASAYANA CHIKITSA)

Tones up the skin and rejuvenates & strengthens all the tissues, so as to achieve ideal health and longevity. Increases 'Ojas' (primary vitality) and improves 'Sattva' (mental clarity) and thereby increases the resistance of the body. Includes head and face massage with medicated oils and creams, body massage with herbal oil or powder, by hand, internal rejuvenative medicines and medicated steam bath. Herbal baths are also used.

Body Immunisation And Longevity Treatment (Kayakalpa Chikitsa):

Prime treatment for retarding the ageing process, arresting the degeneration of body cells and immunisation of the system. Includes intake of Rasayana (special Ayurvedic medicines and diet) and comprehensive body care programs. Most effective for either sex if undertaken before the age of 50.

General Rasayanas

For specific tissues, certain herbs and foods functions as Rasayanas. Some of these are:

Plasma(Rasa)	Draksha, Shatavari, Dates
Blood (Rakta)	Amalki, Dhati lauha, Bhringaraj, Suvarnamakshik Bhasma
Muscle (Mamsa)	Masha, Ashwagandha, Bala, Nux vomica, Silver bhasma
Fat (Meda)	Guggulu, Shilajit, Haritaki, Guduchi, Garlic
Bone (Asthi)	Shukti (mother of pearl) bhasma, Kukku and at wak bhasma, Vamsharochana,
Nerve (Majja)	Calamus, Gotukola, Shankhapushpi, Loha bhasma, Gold bhasma, Makaradhwaja
Reproductive (Shukra)	Kapikacchu, Vidarikanda, Shatavari, Ashwagandha, Gold bhasma, Ghee and Cow milk.
Rasayana for channel-systems:	Certain Herbs and Food functions as Rasayana in specific channel-systems (Srotas).

Respiratory System	Chyavanprash, Vardhaman pippli
Water Metabolism System	Fresh ginger, Cyperus, Cardamom
Digestive System	Long pepper, Bhallataka, Haritaki,
Circulatory System (lymphatic portion)	Draksha, Shatavari, Dates
Circulatory System (blood portion)	Amalki, Dhati lauha, Bhringaraj, Suvarnamakshik Bhasma
Muscular System	Masha, Ashwagandha, Bala, Nux vomica, Silver bhasma
Adipose System	Guggulu, Shilajit, Haritaki, Guduchi, Garlic
Skeletal System	Shukti (mother of pearl) bhasma, Kukkutandatwak bhasma, Vamsharochana,
Nervous System	Ashwagandha, Calamus, Gotukola, Shankhapushpi, Loha bhasma, Gold bhasma, Makaradhwaja
Reproductive System	Ashwagandha, Kapikacchu, Sweta Mushali, Shatavari, Vidarikanda, Gold bhasma, Ghee and Cow milk.
Urinary System	Punarnava, Gokshura
Excretory System	Kutaj, Vidanga, Triphala
Sweat System	Basil, Nux vomica
Menstrual System	Ashoka, Lodhra, Shatavari
Lactation System	Shatavari, Jeeraka, Milk

Rasayana for senses and other organs:

Eye	Triphala, Licorice, Shatavari
Nose	Nasya of Anu oil
Skin	Tuvarak, Catechu, Bakuchi

Brain	Gotu kola, calamus
Heart	Guggul, Elecampane, Gold bhasma
Neuro-Muscular System	Bala, Nagbala, Garlic, Guggul

Rasayana according to constitution:

Vata	Bala, Ashwagandha
Pitta	Amalaki, Shatavari, Guduchi
Kapha	Bhallataka, Guggul, Long pepper, Garlic

KUTIPRAVESIKA

In this process, elaborate arrangements are made for the construction of a special type of cottage where the individual is supposed to stay secluded, while taking the Rasayana. The person has to strictly follow the diets and other instructions of the physician. Here, he undergoes the detoxification process called Panchakarma therapy before taking the rejuvenation. Rejuvenation is done with the help of some specific medicinal formulations and a specific lifestyle regimen. Kaya kalpa is a special rejuvenating method.

The term kaya kalpa means renewal of body. According to ayurveda the human body is made of seven types of dhatu or tissues-structures such as plasma, blood, muscle, fat, bone, marrow and reproductive fluids. To prolong the youthfulness of the body several physical as well as mental disciplinary methods along with rasayanas or herbal medicines are used, to rebuild the body's cells and tissues after the initial process of detoxification—panchakarma.

Kaya kalpa is that unique therapy, which brings about complete rejuvenation of the body through cell and tissue renewal. It is supposed to endow an individual with longevity, memory, intellect, youth, strength of sensory and motor organs, even, an excellent complexion and voice.

VATATAPIKA

This method is best for people who don't have time to stay in the ayurvedic clinic to take the first kind of rejuvenation. It comprises of different types ayurvedic herbal preparations which are taken as prescribed by the doctor. Rasayana is held as the culmination of ayurvedic wisdom.

• • •

4

Characteristics of Vata, Pitta, Kapha

Vata	*Pitta*	*Kapha*
1. Thin and unusually tall of short	1. Medium body.	1. Large body.
2. Light, small bones and/or prominent joints.	2. Medium bone structure	2. Heavy bone structure
3. Long tapering fingers and toes.	3. Fingers and toes medium in length.	3. Fingers and toes short squarish.
4. Thin as a child.	4. Medium build as a child	4. Large or chunky as a child.
5. If gains weight, around middle.	5. If gains weight, deposits fat evenly.	5. Tends to gain-weight, especially on buttocks and thighs.
6. Dark complexion (relative to family tendency).	6. Fair skin, sunbuns easily, freckles and moles common.	6. Tans evenly.
7. Body hair scanty or overabundant,	7. Light body hair fine texture.	7. Moderate amount of body

Vata	Pitta	Kapha
tends to be dark, coarse and curly.		hair.
8. Small forehead folds and lines.	8. Medium forehead.	8. Large forehead.
9. Small, dark, active eyes.	9. Medium size, light green, gray, amber or blue eyes	9. Large, liquid, sometimes blue, often chocolate brown eyes.
10. Crooked, uneven or buck teeth that are sensitive to heat and cold, may have needed braces.	10. Even teeth, of medium size.	10. Large, even, gleaming teeth.
11. Neck small, unsteady.	11. Moderate neck	11. Large, steady neck
12. Delicate chin	12. Moderate chin	12. Large jaw
13. As a child, hair kinky, curly	13. As a child, hair fine light	13. As a child hair wavy & thick

Part II- Characteristics which Change

Vata	Pitta	Kapha
1. Difficulty in gaining weight.	1. Can gain or lose weight if puts mind to it.	1. Gains weight easily, hard time losing without exercise.
2. Cold hands and feet.	2. Skin warm to touch	2. Skin cool but not cold
3. Dry skin (¼"thick pinch skin on touch chaps easily, Prone to corns and callouses.	3. Oily skin, prone to pimples and rashes (¼"-½" thick)	3. Thick skin (¾+" thick), well lubricated

4. Often suffers cracked, chapped lips	4. Deep, red lips, tendency toward cold sores, fever blisters.	4. Full, moist lips.
5. Dry hair, lusterless split ends, dark, rough, wiry or kinky.	5. Fine, light, oily, red or early gray hair, early thinning or baldness possible.	5. Thick, slightly wavy hair, a little oily, dark, brown, lustrous
6. Dislikes dryness and cold (likes warmth).	6. Prefers cool, well ventilated places (dislikes heat).	6. Tolerates most climates (dislikes humidity).
7. Tongue dry with thin grayish coating.	7. Tongue coating yellowish, orange or reddish.	7. Tongue swollen with thick, curdy, white coating.
8. Eyes often dry and scratchy, sclera (whites of eye)	8. Sclera has reddish or yellow tinge	8. Tendency toward eye puffiness.
9. Bowel movement can be irregular, hard dry or constipated.	9. Bowels loose-more then twice a day/ diarrhoea	9. Large full bowel movement, once a day/mucous, itching.
10. If ill: nervous disorders, sharp pain likely	10. If ill: fevers, rashes or inflamation likely.	10. If ill: swelling, fluid retention, mucous, congestion.
11. Sexual interest variable, fantasy life active.	11. Highly sexed, arouses easily.	11. Steedy sex, slow to arouse.
12. Menses irregular, scanty flow, severe painful cramps.	12. May bleed heavily, and long loose stool accompanies period.	12. Prone to water during weight menses slight cramps, if any.
13. Either indulges in rich food or on strict diet.	13. Loves proteins, caffeines & hot, spicy, & salty foods.	13. Loves sweets, dairy bread and pastry.

Vata	Pitta	Kapha
14. Receding gums.	14. Inflamed, bleeding gums.	14. Thick gums.
15. Joints-painful, unsteady, cracking or stiff.	15. Joints-hot, swollen, burning.	15. Joints, loose, aching, watery, swollen.

Part III - Mind

Vata	Pitta	Kapha
1. Concentration is short, short term memory good, but forgets quickly.	1. Good short and long term memory, logical rational thoughts never forgets.	1. Takes time to learn things, once learned
2. Dislikes routine.	2. Enjoy planning organizing especially & routine. if self created.	2. Works well with
3. Difficulty deciding changes mind easily	3. Rapid decision making sees things clearly.	3. Takes time making decisions, sticks with it.
4. Restless, active, likes movement.	4. Aggressive, likes competitive activities.	4. Calm, likes to relax, bleisure activities.
5. Creative thinker.	5. Organized thinker.	5. Prefers to follow a plan or idea.
6. Does many projects all at once orderly fashion.	6. Constantly organizing likes to proceed in	6. Resists projects change new; likes simplicity.
7. Knows a lot of people, few close friends.	7. Very selective, but creates warm friendships/makes enemies easily.	7. Loyal, with many friends

	Vata	Pitta	Kapha
8.	Spends impulsively, money is to be used	Plans spending money is for achieving purpose	Spends reluctantly, likes to save.

Part IV-The Emotions

	Vata	Pitta	Kapha
1.	Experiences fear	Experiences hate	Experiences apathy
2.	Practices Secretiveness	Can be vindictive	Can be uncaring
3.	Can be selfdestructive	Can be destructive	Feels victimized
4.	Anxious	Irritable	Attached
5.	Sneaky	Manipulative	Greedy
6.	Nervous	Angry	Desirous
7.	Dynamic	Perceptive	Harmonious
8.	Communicative	Caring	Devoted
9.	Flexible	Tolerant	Patient
10.	Feelings and emotions change easily	Aggressive about opinions and feelings, gives opinions situations even if they are not asked for	Avoids giving opinions in difficulty
11.	Dreams about flyingrestless, nightmares conflicts	Dreams in color, fast, passion, involve water	Romantic, short dreams, often

• • •

5

Stages of Disease

There are six progressive stages of disease. Disease does not just appear, there is no such thing as a "sudden heart attack." Years of imbalance and neglect create that experience.

The first stage of disease is called accumulation and is begun when there is an imbalance in the doshas and a buildup in the specific areas of the body. This may occur because of inappropriate diet, lifestyle thoughts or feelings.

The second stage, aggravation, is a sign that the dosha has begun to overflow like a bucket of water under a dripping faucet.

The third stage, dissemination, is the excess dosha moving throughout the body. During this stage, there can be a whole range of symptoms occurring in different parts of the body at different times- vague symptoms that are rather hard for the patient or a doctor to pin down.

The fourth stage is known as relocation. This is the stage where the imbalanced dosha has settled into one specific site and begun to cause more serious symptoms.

The fifth stage is manifestation, where the excess dosha has settled down and can now be identified as a specific disease.

The last stage is known as disruption, because the disease manifests, disrupting the health of the individual. It is at this stage that a medical physician can recognize definitely what is wrong and give the disease a name.

∙ ∙ ∙

6

Methods of Preparation of Ayurvedic Medicines

Powder : Dry material in shade. Crush to make fine powder and sieve through a cloth.

Paste: Powder the materials, heat with a little water and make into fine paste or crush the material, add a little water and grind to make a paste.

Fresh Juice: Wash the material (parts or Plant) and remove dirt. Chop the plant into small pieces and crush well. Squeeze the crushed material through a cloth and collect juice.

Decoction: Wash the material (Dry or Fresh) to remove the dirt. Chop into small pieces. Boil ½ cup of material in four cups of water and reduce into one cup. Filter the decoction and use.

Milk Decoction: Wash the material and make it into small pieces and pound it. Boil half cup of it with one cup of milk and four cups of water. Reduce it to one cup. Filter it and use.

The ratio of ingredients is given in each column separately. It should be taken preferably in empty stomach. Any food should be taken only after one hour of taking decoction (Kashaya).

Instructions: Generally all the preparations are for internal use. In other cases special description is given on how to use (external, gargle etc.). When honey, milk, hot water, jaggery, sugar etc. are mentioned as vehicle, it should be taken in sufficient quantity. If the course of medicine is not mentioned it has to be taken till there is relief for the complaint.

Triphala is a group of three fruits namely Haritaki (Harad), Vibhitaki (Baheda), Aamalaki (Aamla), Trikatu consists of three pungents called Pippali, Marich, Sunthi (Dry ginger).

• • •

7

Concepts of Mental Health in Ayurveda

The ancient system of ayurveda (science of life) offers a holistic approach to mental health that integrates the mind, body and soul. Sushruta, the ancient exponent of ayurveda, defines health as svasthya-a state of total biological equilibrium, where the sensory, mental, emotional and spiritual elements are harmoniously balanced. Ayurvedic theory of health is based on tridosha (primary life forces or biological humours). The five elements (panchabhuta) combine in pairs to constitute the three doshas-vata (ether and air), pitta (water and fire) and kapha (water and earth). The combination of these doshas inherited at birth indicates an individual's unique constitution. The dynamic balance of tridoshas creates health.

Ayurveda defines mental health as a state of mental, intellectual and spiritual well-being. "A complete and foolproof definition and interpretation of the mind is impossible to provide...Yet ayurveda has attempted to examine every detail of the mind's attributes with fair success. The concept of health in ayurveda encompasses not only the physical and mental aspects but also the spiritual aspect, which is missing in the modern psychological discourse," says Dr. P. A. Antony of Trichur in Kerala. The ancient classical ayurvedic expert,

Charaka, places the mind in the heart though other texts locate it at the head and the navel. These various views are considered complementary rather than contradictory. The mind is functionally divided into ahankara (ego), ichha (desire, will) and buddhi. Ichha, directed by ahankara, controls the mind. Buddhi, or the intellect, takes the decisions.

The three gunas (sattva, rajas, tamas) are connected to tridosha in ayurveda. According to S. K. Ramachandra Rao, Ayurveda Academy, Bangalore, "The three gunas together are responsible for the existential, experiential, evaluative and transactional dimensions, each of which may serve as a motivational source of stress." The ideal state of mind is sattvic, marked by equanimity. An agitated mind is in the rajasic state, while the lethargic and gloomy mind is in the grips of tamas.

The accumulation of toxins in the body is termed ama. Psychologically, ama arises from holding on to negative emotions and undigested experiences. According to Dr. Deepak Chopra, who has popularized ayurveda worldwide, "The guiding principle of ayurveda is that the mind exerts the deepest influence on the body, and freedom from sickness depends upon contacting our own awareness, bringing it into balance and extending that balance to the body."

Bhutavidya is the special branch of psychiatry in ayurveda dealing with mental diseases. Some scholars interpret 'bhuta' to mean ghosts and spirits who cause abnormal psychological conditions. Others say 'bhuta' represents microscopic organisms like viruses and bacteria. Bhutavidya also examines past life karmic causes, which have no explanation in terms of tridosha. Mental disorders are generally divided into doshonmada (physical basis) and bhutonmada (purely mental basis).

Elements of Ayurvedic Psychology

Charaka in his treatise Charaka Samhita, describes eight essential psychological factors that are negatively affected in various ways in all psychiatric disorders. The psychopathological condition is a function of these factors, which are manas (mind), buddhi, smriti (memory), sajna jnana (orientation and responsiveness), bhakti (devotion), shila (habits), cheshta (psychomotor activity) and achara (conduct). Compared to other major ayurvedic texts like Sushruta Samhita, and Ashtanga Hrdayam, Charaka Samhita gives more emphasis to the view of life as a self-aware field of pure consciousness and natural intelligence where the knower and the known are one.

Signs of Mental Health as per Ayurveda

- Good memory
- Taking the right food at the right time
- Awareness of one's responsibilities
- Awareness of the self and beyond self
- Maintaining cleanliness and hygiene
- Doing theengs with enthusiasm
- Cleverness and discrimination
- Being brave
- Perseverance
- Maintaining cheerfulness irrespective of the situation
- Fearlessness in facing situations
- Sharp intellectual functioning
- Self-sufficiency
- Following a good value system
- Ability to proceed steadfastly against all odds.

Dr. Marc Halpern, founder and director of California College of Ayurveda, Nevada City, California, explains that according to ayurveda, the greatest factor in a person's sensitivity to stress is a substance found within all cellular tissues and the mind, called ojas. Ojas is the vital essence of the immune system and provides the mind with both stability and contentment. The body produces ojas through digesting nourisheeng foods. A nourisheeng diet combined with excellent digestion is the key to building ojas. Ayurveda greatly emphasizes proper digestion. This includes selecting the proper foods for a person's constitution and eating properly. Long-term problems with digestion and elimination deplete ojas, which is protected by instituting a lifestyle that avoids overindulgence, includes sufficient rest and reinforces self-love. Dr. Chopra aptly calls ojas "the bodily counterpart to pure joy." Other essential factors are prana and tejas. Prana is the subtle energy behind all mind/body functions and governs higher states of consciousness. Tejas confers inner radiance and higher perceptual capacities.

Dr. Hemant. K. Singh who served as Scientist at the Government of India's Central Drug Research Institute (CDRI) for thirty years, asserts,"Mental ill health is essentially a result of disequilibrium brought about by unwholesome interaction between the individual and the environment. This interaction operates through an axis consisting of three fundamental factors namely kala (time rhythm), buddhi and indriyata (sense inputs)".

The third classification consists of prakriti or personality disorders. There are sixteen manasa prakriti (psychological personality) representing sixteen types of behavioural traits.

Other conditions are buddhimandya or mental retardation of varying degrees, jara-janya-manasa vikara (psychiatric problems of the aged or gerontological disorders), and manodaihika vyadhis or psychosomatic diseases where the cause of disease is mental but the manifestation is somatic.

Vertigo and other Nervous Disorders

Nervous disorder include headche, vertigo and nervous exhaustion.

For Nervous Disorders

- Mix 1 teaspoon each dried amla powder and coriander seeds (saboot dhania) in water overnight. Strain and drink next morning. To improve the flavour, sugar can be added. Repeat for a few days.
- Heat 2 tablespoon sesame oil (til ka tel). Mix in 1/2 teaspoon each finely powdered cardamom (chhoti illaichi) and cinnamon (dalchini). Apply this on head.
- Mix 7 to 8 almonds with 7 to 8 kernels of pumpkin (kaddu) seeds, 1 teaspoon poppy seeds (Khuskhus) and 3 tablespoons wheat. Soak in water overnight. Next morning, remove the outer skin of the almonds and grind together into a fine paste. Heat separately 2 teaspoons ghee and fry 1/2 teaspoon cloves (laung). Add the paste to it along with some milk and boil the whole mixture. Sweeten with sugar and drink everyday for a few days.

Depression

- Boil 1/4 teaspoon powdered cardamom (chhoti illaichi) seeds in thin tea water and drink.
- Mix 1/8 teaspoon nutmeg (jaiphal) powder with 1 tablespoon freshly extracted amla juice. Take 3 times a day.

NERVOUSNESS

- Apply fresh lime juice on the head. Massage well before showering off.
- Steep 1 tablespoon mint (pudina) leaves in 1 cup water for 30 minutes. Drink the infusion, do not boil.

MEMORY IMPROVEMENT

- Take a mixture of 1 teaspoon honey and a pinch of finely powdered cinnamon (dalchini) every night regularly.
- Take 1/2 teaspoon black cumin (kala jeera) powder and mix it with honey. Eat small quantities of it twice a day.
- Mix 1 teaspoon each amla root powder and white sesame seeds (safed til) powder. Add 1 teaspoon honey and eat everyday for a few days.
- Akhrot & Almonds are good for memory. Take with milk in early morning.

EPILEPSY

- Rub tulsi juice over your body everyday after taking bath.
- Keep the blossoms of tulsi inside the fold of your hanky every time. At the time of attack smell the blossom deeply.
- If the attack makes one unconscious, grind 11 leaves of tulsi, add a little salt to it and put a few drops of this juice in the patient's nostrils. He would immediately regain his consciousness. Keep a tulsi plant in your varanda or somewhere near your bedroom.

HYSTERIA

- If the hysteric effect be due to excess of phlegm in the body, make the patient smell tulsi leaves and drink 5 tulsi leaves juice.

- If it is caused by the excessive heat going to the head, grind five tulsi leaves and five black pepper by mixing them in water and make the patient drink this water every morning and evening for a week's time. Then hysteria will be cured.

Migraine

- Get a small bunch of tulsi blossom, dry in the shade and grind it in powder form. Just take two gms, of it mix about half a spoonful of honey to it and make the person lick it. It is very efficacious treatment. In case you feel like, have another dose for a total cure.

Headache

- Roast some dry ajwain on a tawa. Keep it tightly in a muslin bag and sniff frequently.
- Make a paste of 2-3 powdered cloves (laung) and salt. Apply this paste on the forehead.
- **Tulsi Tea:** Mix 8-10 basil (tulsi) leaves, 1/2" piece ginger (adrak), 7 black pepper corns (saboot kali mirchi) powdered coarsely with 1 large cup (200ml) water. Boil for 2 minutes. Remove from heat, cover and keep for 2-3 minutes. Strain, add boiled milk, sugar and drink warm. Lie down covering yourself with a sheet for 5-10 minutes. It is very helpful in headaches, cold, indigestion. Drink 2-3 times a day. For children reduce quantity to half.
- A ripe apple, after removing the upper rind and the inner hard portion should be taken with a little salt every morning on an empty stomach. Continue for a week. This yields good results even in case of chronic headaches.

- Mix 1 teaspoon finely grind cinnamon (dalchini) in 1 teaspoon water and apply on the forehead. It is very effective in headache due to exposure to cold air.
- Crush an onion and apply the paste on the head.
- Grind 10-15 tulsi leaves with 4 cloves (laung) and 1 teaspoon dried ginger (sonth) into a paste and apply.

HEADACHE ON THE SIDE

- Powder equal quantities of liquorice (mulathi) and cumin (jeera). Take 1/4 teaspoon everyday along with 1 teaspoon honey for a month.
- Mix 1 teaspoon each of the following powders and store: camphor (kapoor), nutmeg (jaiphal), cardamom (chhoti illaichi) and cloves (laung). Take 2 pinches with warm water.

HEADACHE DUE TO EXPOSURE TO COLD AIR

- Mix 1 teaspoon finely grind cinnamon (dalchini) in 1 teaspoon water and apply on the affected parts.

HEAD HEAVINESS

- Grind the fresh amla fruits into a fine paste and apply on affected parts.
- Grind 2 to 3 cloves (laung) into a fine paste along with 1/2 teaspoon dried ginger (sonth) and apply on nose, forehead etc.

HEMICRANIA (ADHASISI)

- When chronic cold makes the extra phlegm block half of the head, this trouble surfaces. Take a smokeless but hot cowdung cake (Upala) and throw grind turmeric powder over it. It will emit large clouds of smoke. Just inhale this smoke which will make you cough and sneeze and all the blocked phlegm will be expectorated through them. Besides, this, put water turmeric's lukewarm solution in the opposite ear you have this trouble in.

•••

8

Disorders of Eyes, Ears and Nose

Eyes, ears and nose are our sense organs. We should take care of these organs.

Eyes Acheeng: When some foreign elements fall in your eyes, like the tiny bits of dust, even if they are removed the eyes ache. Another cause of it is lot of roaming about in the sun without use of the goggles.

- Boil a little of water a bowlful after adding just 10gms. of turmeric to it. When cool, dip a clean soft cloth in this water, wrench the cloth midly to let a few drops go into your affected eyes. When water is pleasantly cool, throw this water on to your eyes and rub it dry by a soft towel. The pain will vanish soon.
- Put a drop of tulsi (Basil) juice mixed with even quantity of honey for a sort of eye troubles, especially pain and burning. This solution can also be preserved in a bottle. If there be the problem of trachoma, grind ten leaves of tulsi together with a clove. Put it into your eyes after every four hours. If there, be swelling in the eyes, add a little of tulsi-juice with alum and apply in your eyes for instant relief.
- Powder equal quantities of liquorice (mulathi) and cumin (jeera). Take ½ teaspoon every day along with 1 teaspoon honey for a month.

Eyes Strain due to TV Watcheeng:

- Boil ½ teaspoon fennel seeds (saunf) in a cup of water till it is reduced to half and cool it. Use as eye drops

CAUTION: BEWARE OF CONTAMINATION.

Eyes Tired

- Lavender oil offers gentle relief for tired and strained eyes. Add a drop of lavender oil to 500ml (2½ cups) of water and shake the solution well. Dip two cotton wool pads in the liquid, squeeze out the excess water and place them over each eye. If you wear contact lenses, they must be removed before doing this.

Eyes Burning

- Mash 1 ripe banana along with a little curd and water, take twice a day.
- Mix equal quantities of fenugreek seed (methi daana) powder along with Shikakai powder for washeeng hair. Wash frequently.
- Grind an onion with 1 teaspoon each black pepper and poppy seeds soak in ½ cup milk. Apply this paste on the head. Allow it to dry for 15-20 minutes. Wash with warm water.
- Mix the juice of bottle gourd and sesame oil (til ka tel) in the ratio of 4:1 and heat till the moisture is evaporated completely. Once cool, use it for massaging the head.

Eyes Sore

- Take a large lemon (bijora or galgal), make a whole into it and put a piece of turmeric in this cavity. In just two weeks time the lemon would be derived up and the turmeric piece would have sucked its juice. Now dry the turmeric in shade and grind it finely so that it may be strained through a fine cloth. Turn up the eyelids having this sore and rub lightly this powder. In just two days, all the eye sores will be cured and your eyes will become normal.

CATARACT

The beginning of the cataract formation in the eye results in the sight failing. The affected one feels as if he is seeing through a glass. The cataract continues to get matured and the sight continues to fall. When it is fully mature, it is removed by surgical operation.

- Take 10 gms. of the juice of onions, good quality of honey 10 gms, and Bhimseni camphor (kapoor) 2 gms. Make a homogeneous mixture of the three and preserve them in a bottle. Every night before you go to sleep, apply it in your eyes by a eye liner. Its regular use prevents the cataract formation.

CATARACT, EARLY STAGE

- Mix 1 teaspoon rose water (gulab jal) with 1 teaspoon fresh lime juice. Add 10 drops of this to the eyes.
- Extract the juice of tulsi and add a little of honey to it. Apply this over the eyes every morning and evening. If the cataract be of raw type, it shall be cut away and if it be of ripe type, it shall be ripened soon to enable the doctor to remove it by operation.

EYE SIGHT FAILING:

Take equal quantity of turmeric and the soft neem sprouts. Grind both of them in a handy stone crusher with the milk of the peepal added to it. Grind the lot for five days pouring in fresh peepal milk everyday. From the 7th day onwards you can start using this paste like collyrium to line your eyes with. In just four weeks time your eye sight will not only stop fall, it will begin to improve as much as to make your reading glasses redundant.

- Stop reading at all in dim light or reading while lying down. Don't have very hot or very cold drinks. Eat easily digestible and nourisheeng food. Keep your bowels clean. Use the following powders:
- Take cumin seeds and coriander seeds in equal measure and sieve through a thin, clean cloth. Then take "Khand" in equal measure and grind the three again to a powdered form. Have about 10 gms. of this powder everyday in the evening and morning with fresh water. Wash your eyes with cold clean water.

Eyesight Weakness

- Mix seeds of cardamom (chhoti illaichi) along with 1 tablespoon honey. Eat every day.
- Boil 2 tablespoons fenugreek (methi) leaves along with 1/2 cup moong dal and 10 small onions and eat regularly.
- Mix equal quantities of fenugreek seeds (methi daana) powder along with shikakai powder for washeeng hair. Wash your hair frequently.

Dark Circles Around Eyes

- Take one teaspoon tomato juice, 1/2 teaspoon lemon juice, a pinch of turmeric (haldi) powder & a little gram flour (besan). Make a paste & apply. Leave for 10 minutes & wash off.
- Drink tomato juice with a few mint leaves, little lemon juice & salt.

Disorders of Eyes, Ears and Nose

- Soak cotton wool in cucumber (kheera) or potato juice & apply around the eyes. You will find a change in 2-3 weeks.

NIGHT BLINDNESS

- The patients of this disease can't see anytheeng in the dark. It can be caused by prolonged fever or continued undernourishment. Normally this trouble surfaces at the end of the rainy season. If it is not cured in six months time, it becomes rather chronic.
- The basic line of remedy is to feed the patient on easily digestible but nourisheeng diet. Regular use of milk, butter cream, half boiled eggs, green vegetables and fresh sweet vegetables are very effective to fight this ailment. If the constipatory tendency is there then administering the Murabba of 'Harh' together with 25 gms. of gulkand is very effective. Dropping the onion juice in the effected eyes for about a week (just two drops twice daily is very effective.

OTHER EYE TROUBLES

Eye wounds: Take a thick piece of turmeric and grind it on a clean stone like you grind sandalwood. Take this paste on your eye liner and put it in your eyes. The wounds will heal up soon. After applying this special paste, wash your eyes with lukewarm water after half an hour of the application. In the night, when you go to sleep, dip a cloth piece in turmeric boiled water after cooling it, and wrench the cloth to pour few drops every night over the eyes before you retire to bed. You can keep the cloth over your eyes for better relief.

EYE WEB

- Boil about half kg. water with a pinchful of alum and half spoonful turmeric powder added to it. Now cool this water.

Drench a cloth piece in this water and put it over your eyes. When this water is bearable warm, wrench this cloth to drop few drops of this water direct into your eyes. Do so in the evening and morning. In about ten days time the webs will be dissolved.

EYE PUPIL OUTGROWTH (PHULI)
- Take a heavy piece of turmeric, 10 gms. dry leaves of neem and 10 gms. of black pepper. Grind them in a kharal after mixing adequate quantity of cow's urine.
- Everyday add fresh urine of cow and continue grinding it for six days. On the seventh day, add a little of rose water and a piece of camphor. Now your surma is ready. Keep it as it is for three days more and start to line your eyes with the surma every evening and morning. Soon the outgrowth will be dissolved and your eye sight will also improve.

TRACHOMA

In this trouble the upper eyelid has some protruding growth which hurt the eye, causing it to grown and full of irritation.
- **Remedy:** Take 'rasout' 10 gms., Turmeric 3gms., alum 3gms., rose water 10 gms-soak all of them in a glass vessel overnight. And in the morning strain the solution through a thick cloth. Then fill in your eyes with the help of a dropper. In a week's time the trouble will vanish.

EYES OOZING WATER VOLUNTARILY

This is a common ailment in which without any apparent trouble eyes continue to shed water.
- **Remedy:** Take 2 rattis of alum and dissolve it in a tola (a little more than 10 gms.) of rose water, soak cotton wad in

this solution and put it over the eyes at least twice daily preferably first in the morning and then when you retire to bed.

Ear, Boils Inside:

- Heat 2 teaspoons mustard oil. Add ½ teaspoon carom (ajwain) seeds and one or two flakes of crushed garlic (lahsan). Boil till they turn red. Filter it. Use as ear drops.

Ear Pain due to Boils

- Heat 1 teaspoon each of garlic (lahsan) and carom seeds (ajwain) in 2 teaspoons mustard oil. When the garlic becomes brown, remove the oil from fire and cool it. Pour two drops in the acheeng ear.
- If there is swelling in the ears, then add the juice of bhanga with the juice of black tulsi and put a few drops of this juice inside the affected or both the ears for quick relief.

Ear Infections

- Extract 1 teaspoon juice from mango leaves. Slightly warm and use as ear drops when bearably hot.

Earache

- Heat 2 teaspoons mustard oil. Add ½ teaspoon carom seeds (ajwain) and one or two flakes of crushed garlic (lahsan). Boil till they turn red, filter it. Use as ear drops.
- Boil well 1 teaspoon lahsan (garlic) in 2 tablespoons ginger oil (til ka tel). Cool and filter. Use as ear drops (1 to 3 drops).
- Mix a few drops of lime juice in 1 teaspoon lukewarm water. Put 4 drops of this into the ear.
- Use neem leaves juice as ear drops.

- Take radish leaves, put them in 25 gms. of mustard oil and cook it slowly. Boil them as much as to reduce the watery content of the leaves to naught. When cold, strain and put it in a clean bottle. First of all, dip a cotton bud in this oil and clean your ears with it. Then drop a few drops of this oil. It is better if you do it by night when you retire to bed.
- Take about 10 leaves of makoy and ten leaves of tulsi. Extract their juice together and put it in the affected ear when it is slightly lukewarm (heat it a little in the sun). Alternatively add half a tablet of camphor in tulsi juice and put this juice in the ear for instant relief.
- If lukewarm basil leaves juice is dropped in the affected ear, this remedy brings immediate relief.
- Take out the juice of marigold flower's leaves, heat it a little and put it just two drops at a time twice daily.
- Take out the extract of beetroot leaves, heat it a little and drop just two to three drops in the affected ear.
- Make water saline by dissolving 'Sendha Namak' into it. Put a few drops daily morning and evening.
- Mix honey in the ginger juice with salt. Heat it a little and put two drops in the affected ear.

Ear Oozing Fluid

- 20 gms. of alum, turmeric 1 gm., grind both of them to a fine powder form and keep the powder in the bottle. Before using the powder, clean the ear thoroughly with a cotton bud. Then get this powder blown in the affected ear just 5gms., of it every time. A few days regular use will cure the trouble.
- Heat a bit the juice of onion and drop two drops of it in the affected ear. This is an ideal remedy for all the ear troubles.

Ear Trouble (Pus Formation)

- To clear out the pus, take two pieces of turmeric and roast them in the mustard oil. Now strain the oil and fill it in a clean bottle. Pour either a few drops of this oil into the ear or clean the inside with the help of cotton buds dipped in this oil. In a fortnight the pus formation will stop and your hearing power shall also be enhanced.

Deafness

If the trouble is congenital or caused by some external injury, it can't be cured. But if it is caused by some internal disturbance in the ear, then it can certainly be cured by the following treatment:

- Take a swallow leaf of the plant of swallow worf. See that it has no holes. Heat it on fire a little and then extract its juice and drop it into the affected ear. About two weeks regular treatment can cure the ailment. Even the wound in the ear can also be cured by this treatment.
- Drop a few drops of lukewarm juice of onion into the ear. Onion juice is good for all the ear ailments. Even the similar use of bitter almonds can cure the ailment.
- Use raw onion juice as ear drops.
- Put two drops of lukewarm neem oil inside the ear.

Nose Blockage due to Cold and Phlegm

- Make into a very fine powder equal quantities of the following : green cardamom (chhoti illaichi) seeds, cinnamon (dalchini), black pepper (kali mirch) and cumin seeds (jeera). Sniff this powder frequently to induce sneezing.

Nose Running

- Rub a nutmeg (jaiphal) on a smooth grinding stone along with some cow's milk. Apply this paste on forehead and nose.

Sneezing

- Boil 2 tablespoon fennel seeds (saunf) in 1 cup water till it is reduced to half. Filter it. Take 1 tablespoon every morning and evening for a few days.

Sinus

- Take a smokeless but burring cow dung cake and sprinkle turmeric powder over it. It will emit large quantities of smoke. Inhale this smoke deeply. It will release the stuck up solid phlegm in the nose and the patient will be cured.

Cold with Phlegm (Balgam) and Slight Cough

- Take 8-10 tulsi leaves and wash them well. In the 1 cup of water, add these tulsi leaves, 1-2 cloves of garlic (lahsan), ½ piece ginger, crushed and 4-5 peppercorns (saboot kali mirch). Boil the water and keep simmering on fire till the quantity is reduced to ¼ cup. Cool it. Strain the potion and add 1 teaspoon honey. Drink this every morning.

Nose Bleeding

- Take a big piece of turmeric and grind it with half kilo of dried bansa leaves. Add 25 gms. rock salt. Boil the lot in water till the quantity is reduced one fourth of the original quantity. Strain the potion and cool it. Take just 10gms. of it at one hourly interval just sip the potion. In a couple of hours the extra heat of the blood shall pass out with urine and the nose bleeding will stop. Externally make the patient smell a cotton wet with the itra of khus for quick relief.
- Drop lemon juice in nostrils.
- Use juice of fresh coriander leaves (dhania) as nasal drops.

Disorders of Eyes, Ears and Nose

- Dip a cotton bud in rosewater and dab it on to the inside of your nostrils to stop the bleeding.

NOSE BLEEDING DUE TO BODY HEAT:

- Lemon juice dropped into nostrils provides excellent relief.
- Juice of fresh coriander leaves (dhania) can be used as nasal drops.
- The easiest and most effective cure of this trouble is to keep the tulsi blossom near you and smell it as and when you like. For those who are chronic patient of this trouble, this simple treatment is very effective and cures the trouble almost totally. Drinking tulsi juice mixed with honey will also help and provide extra strength to the body.
- Take 10gms. of fuller's earth and keep it in a cup full of water. When the process of sedimentation has taken place, drink the water early in the morning from the cup.
- Take a little of dry 'Aanwala' and soak it in about 25 gms. of water. Sieve through a fine cloth and drink the strained water early in the morning. The remaining material should be grinded to a paste form and be applied over palate and forehead.
- Grind 'Majufal' to fine powdered form and ask the patient to smell it repeatedly. The bleeding from the nose shall stop.

COLD & COUGH

- The chronic patients of this problem have their hair going untimely white. To stop the process and cure it, take 300gms. of tulsi leaves dried in shade, 50 gms. of Dalchini, 100gms. Tejpat, 200gms. Saunff (anise seeds), 200gms of small cardamom, Agiya 300 gms; Banfshaw 25 gms; red sandal 200gms. and Brahmi herb 200 gms., grind all these ingredients and strain them through a cloth. Now take

10 gms. of this powder, boil it in 500gms. water and when just a cup of this water remains, add sugar and milk and drink it twice a day like you have tea. All these problems will vanish in a couple of days.
- A tablespoon of carom seeds crushed and tied up in a muslin cloth can be used for inhalation to relieve congestion/blocked nose.
- A similar small bundle carom seeds placed near the pillow of sleeping children relieves congestion.
- A teaspoon of cumin seeds is added to 1 glass of boiling water. Strain and simmer for a few minutes. Let it cool. Drink it 1-2 times a day. If sore throat is also present, add a few small pieces of dry ginger to the boiling water.
- Six pepper corns finely grind and mixed with a glass of warm water, sweetened with 5-6 batasha can be taken for a few nights.
- In the case of the acute cold in the head, boil 1 tablespoon pepper powder in a cup of milk along with a pinch of turmeric (haldi) and have once daily for at least 3 days.
- A lemon a day keeps the cold away. For a bad cold, the juice of two lemons in ½ a litre (2½ cups) of boiling water sweetened with honey, taken at bed time, is a very effective remedy.
- Have ginger (adrak) tea. Cut ginger (adrak) into 1-1½ pieces and boil with a cup of water. Give 8-10 boils. Strain, sweeten with ½ teaspoon sugar and drink hot.

NASAL CONGESTION

- Crush a fistful of carom seeds (ajwain) and tie up in a cotton napkin and place it near the pillow.
- Put 1 teaspoon cardamom (chhoti illaichi) seeds on burning coal and inhale the smoke.

Nasal Congestion in Children

- Crush a fistful of carom seeds (ajwain) and tie up in a cotton napkin and place it near the pillow.

Foul Smeling Nose

Many person have this trouble. It is due to stomach disorder of the person. The following treatment is found to be quite effective.

- Grind the bitter pumpkin to a paste form and extract its juice. Drop two three drops of this pumpkin juice in the patient's nose. If you don't get fresh bitter pumpkin then you can take already dried pumpkin and soak it in water overnight. Grind it to a paste form early in the morning and drop this paste's juice in the sufferer's nose every morning. Besides this treatment, try to keep your digestive system in perfect order.

• • •

9

Disorders of Throat, Mouth and Teeth

Mouth, throat and teeth are the part of our oral hygiene. We should not any pain or ulcer of this area.

Sore Throat

- Apply liquorice mulathi paste around the throat for relief.
- Eat a plain betel leaf (pan) with liquorice (mulathi) 2-3 times a day.
- Drink tea boiled with ginger (adrak) and a few tulsi leaves 2-3 times a day
- Gargle with warm salt at least twice a day. However do not make gargling sounds as this may aggravate the soreness.
- Pound 2-3 cloves (laung), garlic (lahsan) and add to a cupful of honey. Keep for 1-2 days. have one teaspoon thrice a day.
- Drink lots of water (10-12 glasses) everyday, since most throat problems are intensified by dehydration.
- Have the mixture of ½ teaspoon honey and ½ teaspoon lemon juice every 1-2 hours.

Disorders of Throat Mouth and Teeth

Throat Pain

- Crush a few neem leaves with water. Remove pulp. Warm it up. Add a little honey and gargle three or four times a day.
- Mix 1 teaspoon lime juice and 1 tablespoon honey. Swallow tiny amounts slowly 2-3 times a day.

Throat Hoarseness

- Soak 8 to 10 almonds overnight in 1 cup water. After discarding the outer skin, grind the kernels with 8 to 10 black pepper (saboot kaali mirch) in 1 cup water. Sift it and drink once a day, after adding sugar candy (mishri) to taste.
- Take 1 teaspoon onion juice mixed with 1 teaspoon honey.
- Pour 1 glass boiling water on a mixture of 1 teaspoon each of crushed cinnamon sticks (dalchini) and green cardamoms (chhoti illaichi). Keep aside. Filter and use as a gargle when warm.
- Boil 2 teaspoons fennel seeds in barley water and take twice or thrice a day.

Hoarse Voice

- Mix seeds of green cardamom (chhoti illaichi) along with 1 tablespoon honey. Eat everyday.
- Add 2 tablespoon of fenugreek seeds to 6 cups of water. Heat on low flame for 15-20 minutes. Cool to bearable temperature. Strain and gargle with this, 2-3 times a day.
- Heat a cup of milk till warm. Add 1-2 pinches of turmeric powder (Haldi), mix well and drink at night.
- Just extract the juice of 10 tulsi leaves, add a little of honey and lick it. Just a small spoonful quantity of this solution

will soothe your throat nerves and your voice will be again sweet.

Mouth Infection

- Powder dried mint (pudina). Use as toothpowder.

Mouth Inflammation

- Soak 1 tablespoon crushed liquorice (mulathi) root in 2 cups of water for 2 to 3 hours and use it for gargling frequently.

Bad Odour

- Use neem twigs as toothpaste.
- Powder the dried mint (pudina) leaves. Use as toothpowder.
- Boil some cinnamon (dalchini) in a cup of water. Store it in a clean bottle in your bathroom. Use it as a mouth wash frequently.
- Parsley leaves are rich in chlorophyll, nature's own deodoriser. Chew some leaves regularly and your breath will remain fresh. Alternatively, you can chew some cardamom seeds (illaichi) to sweeten your breath. Chew some fennel seeds frequently.
- Chew a piece of cinnamon (dalchini) put in a betel leaf (paan ka patta).
- Tea made by boiling 1 teaspoon fenugreek seeds (methi dana) taken twice or thrice a day. A little honey or lemon juice can be added to improve the flavour.

Mouth Ulcers (Apathae)

- Chew one or two tender leaves of fig (angeer) and leaf buds frequently and wash the mouth with warm water.

God of Ayurveda

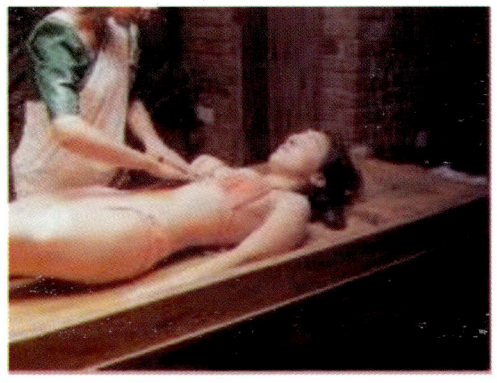

Oil Treatment

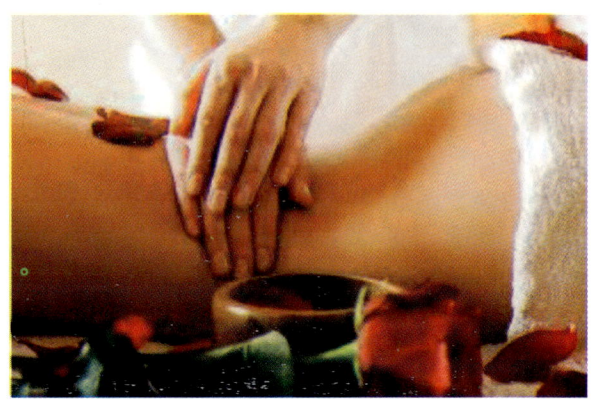

Oil Treatment on Back

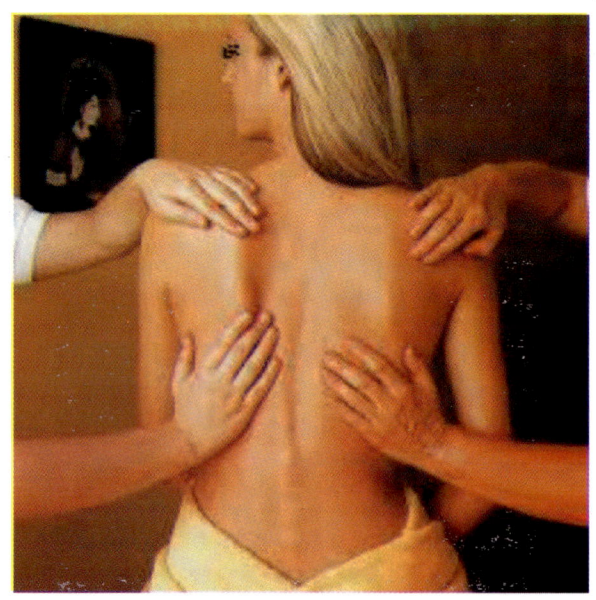

Massage on Back

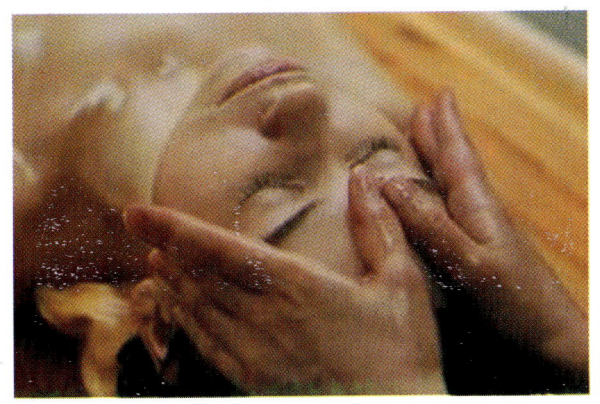

Massage on Forehead

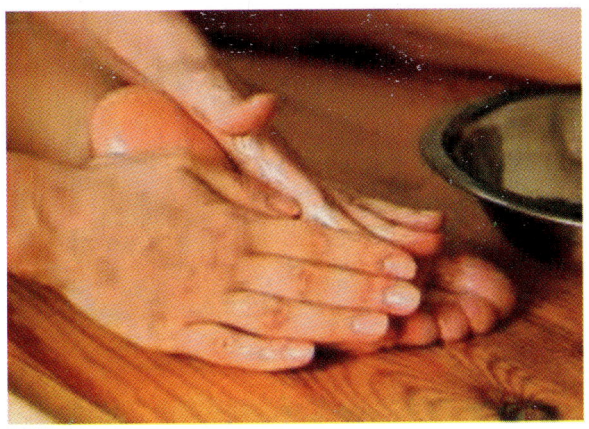

Foot Massage

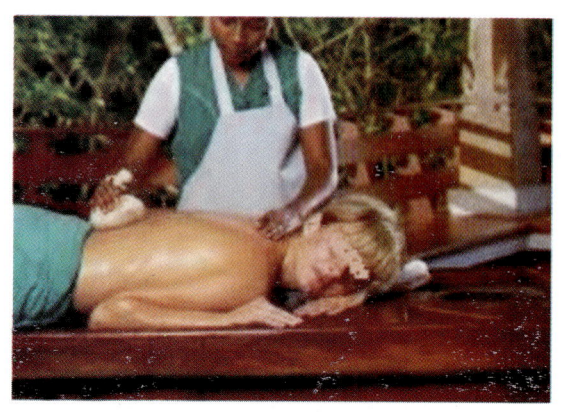

Potali Massage

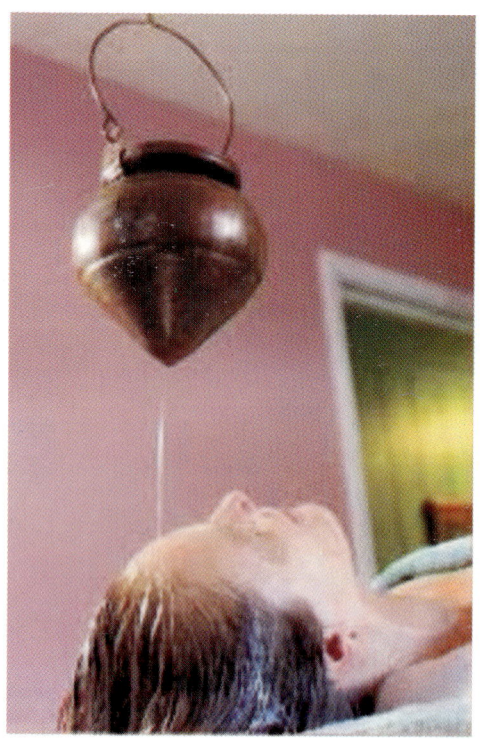

Shirodhara

Another Type of Shirodhara

Herbal Pedicure

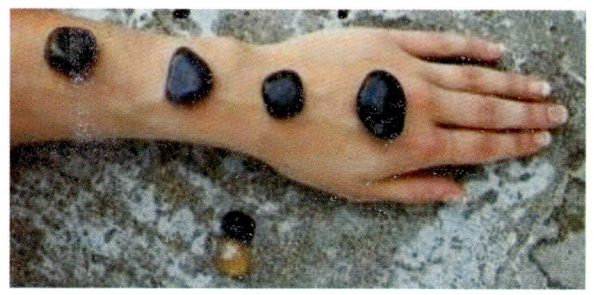

Stone Massage

Home Herbs

Plant Products

Spices

Food

Cleansing Chakras

- Soak 1 tablespoon crushed liquorice (mulathi) root in 2 cups of water for 2 to 3 hours and use it for gargling frequently.
- Boil 2 tablespoons fenugreek (methi) leaves along with ½ cup green gram (saboot moong dal) and 10 small onions. Eat regularly.
- Fenugreek seeds(methi dana), fried and powdered. This is added to drinking water. Drink 2-3 times daily for 2-3 days.
- Pour boiling water over fenugreek (methi) leaves. Keep aside till lukewarm. Strain and gargle with this infusion, 5-6 times daily for a couple of days.
- Mix some coconut milk with honey and massage the gums 3 to 4 times a day.
- Gargle with (or apply) freshly extracted coconut milk from a ripe coconut frequently.
- Mix the pulp of a ripe bel fruit with jaggery (gur) and eat once a day.
- Mix tea cup bel pulp with 1 teaspoon sugar and eat early morning on an empty stomach for 3 days.
- Prepare coriander (dhania) decoction by boiling 1 teaspoon coriander seeds (saboot dhania) in 1 cup water and gargle frequently, when lukewarm.

Mouth Boils

- Take just a leaf of Chameli plant, and four leaves of tulsi. Chew them properly for a few minutes and suck in the juice. In about a day the trouble will vanish.

Teeth Disorders

- Teeth are very vital factors in the process of digestion because it is they which first deal with the food one eats.

These teeth are of quite different varieties. Some cut the food, some munch it and some press it with the help of saliva. Teeth are important not only to help indigestion but also to keep the face beautiful.

TOOTHACHE AND INFIRMITY OF TEETH

- Take 10 gms. of pippali churna, sendha namak 10 gms, grind them to a powdered form and use this combination as the tooth powder to clean your teeth.
- In case of toothache, rub a little of honey over your teeth and allow the saliva to flow out of the mouth. If your teeth has a worm or cavity then fill it with the above mentioned powder and then rinse your mouth.
- Take ammonium chloride 5 gms. and put it by means of a cotton wad to the affected teeth. Allow saliva to ooze out. The toothache shall vanish soon.
- Heat 1 teaspoon coconut oil and fry 3 pieces of cloves (laung) powder. Apply on the affected area.
- Apply nutmeg oil in affected parts.
- Burn the shells of almonds and powder it. Use as toothpowder. •Soak a piece of cotton wool in a few drops of clove oil. Press on affected areas.
- Paste of dry ginger (saunth) apply to gums alongwith a little salt.
- Apply a mixture of powdered black pepper (kali mirch) and clove oil on the affected part.
- Pour some asafoetida (heeng) in a mortar & pestle and add some lime juice. Heat it slightly. Soak a piece of cotton and hold it on the affected area.
- Take three gms of turmeric, three cloves and three dried leaves of guava. Boiling them in 250 gms. of water and after straining it through a fine sieve, rinse your mouth

with this lukewarm water for about 15 minutes. You could get instant relief. Alternatively, roast a turmeric piece in hot ash and then press the turmeric by your acheeng teeth. Do so for two minutes and then the saliva come out of your mouth. Spit it away. Soon the trouble will vanish.

TOOTH YELLOW

- Mix salt with finely powdered rind of lime (nimbu ka chilka). Use this as toothpowder frequently.
- Burn the shells of almonds and powder. Use as toothpowder.

FILTHY TEETH

- Burn an oyster shell to ashes, add a little of salt, grind and sieve through a fine cloth and preserve the powder for rubbing it over the teeth.
- Take about 50gms, of keekarwood, roasted alum 20 gms and Namak Lahori 10 gms, grind and sieve the whole mixture and rub this powder over your teeth every morning and evening.

TEETH WEAKNESS

- Burn to ashes a piece of turmeric, grind it with Bishop's weed (ajwain) and use this mixed powder as your tooth powder. Continuing cleaning your teeth with this powder would provide relief in a couple of week's time. When you apply this powder to your teeth, allow the saliva to ooze out for a few minutes before rinsing your mouth. But, avoid taking very hot drinks and stop consuming sweets in excessive quantity. Sweets especially the white cleaned sugar is very bad for the teeth, just avoid it.

TOOTH DECAY

- Take a piece of turmeric, roast it and then grind it to powder form. Then fill this powder in the cavity caused by tooth decay. In case you are unable to sleep owing to toothache caused by the decay in teeth or tooth, then grind turmeric, bishop's weeds and cloves and tie them in a small piece of cloth. Put this cloth below the acheeng teeth press it mildly and let the teeth get the essence of these ingredients. As you ooze the saliva out your toochache will vanish with it.

•••

10

Disorders of Respiratory System

Respiration is our prana. We should exhale and inhale properly. We should learn pranayama and other breatheeng exercises from an yoga expert.

COUGH WITH PHLEGM (BALGAM)

- Mix equal amounts of onion juice & honey. Have 1 teaspoon 3-4 times a day. This is a preventive medicine against cold in winter.

COUGH (DRY)

- Nearly 250gms. of sweet apples should be taken daily for a week to obtain relief.
- A glass of warm water with juice of 1 lime and 1-2 teaspoon of honey is very good for cough.
- Mix 8-10 tablespoons of coconut milk with 1 tablespoon poppy seeds (khuskhus) and 1 tablespoon pure honey. Take every night before going to bed.
- Mix equal amounts of honey and ginger (adrak) juice for better results, warm the mixture a little & then have it. Have 1 teaspon, 2-3 times a day.
- Three pepper corns (saboot kali mirch) sucked with a pinch of black cumin (shah jeera) and a pinch of salt gives relief.

- Mix 1 teaspoon pepper powder with 4 teaspoon gur (Jaggery). Make small balls. Suck 3-4 balls/tablets during the day.
- Mix equal amounts of pepper powder and sugar candy (mishri) by weight, mix enough pure ghee to form .
- Small balls. Suck one ball/tablet 3-4 times a day. Avoid curd, bananas, ice, rice, fried and cold foods.
- Give 1 teaspoon of basil (tulsi) leaves juice, 2-3 times a day to children having cough. Tulsi leaves can be crushed to a paste and the paste squeezed through a clean muslin cloth to get juice.
- Mix a pinch of turmeric (haldi) with warm 1 cup milk and have at night.

WHOOPING COUGH

- Take about 10gms. of tulsi leaves and even amount of black pepper. Now grind them together to homogeneous powder form. Now adding a little of honey to the combination and make small tablets. These astringent tasting tablets should be taken at least four times a day. Don't swallow these tablets but suck them slowly.
- If the accompanying cough be of dry type, add a little of honey then additionally, make the patient have the combined juice extracted from the even amount of tulsi seeds, ginger and onion. In case of wet cough add sugar candy also in the combination.
- Crush about 50 gms. of radish in your house and add equal amount of sugarcane juice. It would be advisable to add a piece of ginger's juice also in the concoction. Have this combination at least twice a day for speedier relief.
- Radish is a very tasty and useful vegetable and must form the part of everyone's diet. Another root, which is also full of medicinal qualities and equally tasty is carrot.

- A child suffering from this trouble should do away from all foods which produce phlegm like milk, ghee, sweets, rice, refined flour products, sugar and lentils. Give the child citrous but sweet fruits. Some tested remedies are given below:-
- Burn the plantain leaves to ashes and ask the child to lick about 5gms. of this ash daily. In about two weeks time this trouble shall be over.
- If the child is also afflicted with constipation, make him lick the combination of pure honey 6gms. and castor - oil 6gms; followed by the combination of cumin seeds, liquorice, munnekka 3, boiled in water, mixed with pure honey.
- Chew a clove (laung) with a pinch of salt to ease expectoration and relieve irritation in throat.
- Pour 1 cup boiling water over 1/2 teaspoon each of ginger powder, clove powder and cinnamon powder. Filter it. Sweeten with 1 teaspoon honey and drink.

ASTHMA

- Extract about 200gms. of carrot juice and add about 100gms. of spinach juice with it. Have this combined juice at least thrice a day for getting relief. But one must continue this treatment at least for three months for its total cure. Have carrot and spinach also as salad in addition.
- An expectorant and a very effective remedy for asthma is prepared by boiling 6 cloves (laung) in 3 tablespoons of water. Take 1 teaspoon of this decoction with a little honey, thrice daily.
- Mix equal amounts of fresh ginger (adrak) juice, honey & pomegranate (annaar) juice. Take 1 tablespoon, 1-2 times a day.

- Figs are known to give relief by draining the phlegm (balgam). Take 3-4 dry figs, wash them well with warm water. Soak overnight in a cup of water. Eat them first in the morning and also drink the water. Do this for at least 2 months.
- Take 'Alshi' (10 gms) and after coarsely grinding it, boil in about 250gms. of water. When water remains half due to evaporation, add 20 gms. of honey to it. Honey is a very effective expectorant.
- Juice of onions 50gms; the juice of gwarpathe 50 gms; ginger juice 50gms. and pure honey 10gms. Mix them all in a glass container. Close it with the lid and dig it underground for 72 hours. Then take it out and let the patient lick it 6gms. each time, at least twice daily, preferably in the morning and evening.
- If available then take indigenous wax, resin and ghee . Mix the three and put it over the live charcoal. The smoke emitted by the mixture should be inhaled deeply by the patient of asthma. This smoke clears the chest congestion and relieves the tension in the lungs.
- Mix 1 teaspoon honey with 1/2 teaspoon cinnamon powder and have it at night before going to bed.
- Boil carom seeds in water and inhale the steam.
- Boil 8-10 flakes of garlic (lahsan) in 1/2 cup of milk. Have this every night. It gives excellent results in early stages of asthma.
- Add a handful of drumstick leaves to 1 cup water. Boil, simmer on low flame for 3-4 minutes. Cool and strain. Add salt, pepper and lemon juice to taste. Have everyday, once or twice a day.
- Mix 1/4 teaspoon asafoetida, 2 teaspoons honey, 1/2 teaspoon juice from betel leaf (paan ka patta) 1/2 teaspoon

white onion juice. Have it 2-5 times a day. To take out juice from betel, crush to a paste and squeeze through a clean muslin cloth. For onion juice, grate the onion and squeeze through a clean muslin cloth.

BREATHEENG PROBLEM

- Mix 1 teaspoon camphor (kapoor) in 1/2 cup slightly warm coconut oil and apply on the chest.
- Boil 2 tablespoon fennel seeds (saunf) in 1 cup water till it is reduced to half. Filter it. Take 1 tablespoon every morning evening for a few days.
- Boil 3 tablespoon powdered nutmeg (jaiphal) in 1 cup sesame oil (til ka tel). Cool it and apply on affected parts.
- Mix 1 teaspoon oil of garlic (lahsan) & 3 teaspoons honey and take a small amount three times a day.

CHEST CONGESTION

- Add to 1/2 litre of boiling water, 1 teaspoon carom seeds powder along with 1 teaspoon turmeric powder. Cool it and take 1 tablespoon of this mixture alongwith 1 teaspoon honey.

CHEST CONGESTION CAUSING BREATHEENG PROBLEM

- Grind 1/4 teaspoon mustard seeds (sarson) to a smooth paste. Mix with honey and eat.
- Mix equal quantities of mustard powder and rice flour. Add some water and boil until it reaches a paste like consistency. Spread on a handkerchief and foment the chest and neck when bearably hot.

PNEUMONIA

- Get the pure tulsi oil from a recognised Ayurvedic medicine shop. Put this oil on the chest of the afflicted person.

Together with this treatment, extract the juice of five tulsi leaves, mix it with a few grind grains of black pepper at 6 hourly interval. This combined treatment will produce enough heat in the body to make the person sweat. With sweat all the effect of cold inside the body shall vanish and the patient will be cured.

- Take a thick cloth and make four folds of it. Between the third and fourth fold, spread a layer of turmeric. Now mix turmeric in lukewarm water and sprinkle over the cloth to make it partially wet. Now put this cloth on the chest of the patient, heat a brick and put it over the chest of the patient to foment his chest, when the heat from the brick reaches your chest, it would nullify the pneumonia effect. Also take one gm. of black pepper, five cloves and one gm. of edible soda. Boil it in 15gms. of water. When it is drinkable, make the patient sip it for early relief.

•••

Part – II

11

Disorders of Digestive System

The root of the most of the diseases is stomach. We should avoid constipation and acidity by checking the wrong eating habits.

STOMACH PAIN AROUND NAVEL

- Grind 2 teaspoon carom seeds and dried ginger into a fine powder. Add a little black salt (kala namak). Take 1 teaspoon of this mixture with warm water frequently.

ACIDITY

- The best way to treat this trouble is to have lots of fresh radishes. For taste you may add carrots and tomatoes but not salt. The chlorine discharged by radish is very effective to clear the extra acidic contents from the blood. If you like, you must add a little of rock salt to make it more tasty. Drinking juice of radish would also be very helpful. But drinking this juice immediately after extracting it because the gas it has gets lost when kept for long.
- Chewing a piece of harad is an age old remedy.
- Drink coconut water 3-4 times a day.
- Have a plateful of watermelon (tarbooz) and/or cucumber (kheera) every hour.

- Harad juice, 1-2 teaspoon daily after meals is very effective in controlling acidity. The juice can be mixed with an equal amount of amla juice for better results. To take out amla juice, grate an amla and squeeze the pulp through a clean muslin cloth to get juice.
- Take a tiny piece of jaggery (gur) every hour. Just keep it in the mouth and slowly suck it till acidity subsides.
- Take dried blossom of tulsi, rind of the Neem tree, black pepper and peepal in even quantity and grind them to powder form. Take 3 gms of this powder every morning and evening with plain water. All the acidic effect of the body shall pass out with urine and sweat, but remember, never to take milk over tulsi leaves which might afflict your skin.

Dyspepsia & Indigestion

- Sometimes continued irregular food intake and heavily spiced food create a positive dislike for food. Radish has not only the quality of clearing the bowels but it is a very good appetiser also. Have its pieces as much as you want, after properly adding rock salt and lemon. At this state, drinking, radish juice would not be as effective as to have raw radish, skip your meal and have only salads soon you'd long for food.
- Boil 5-6 sticks of powdered cinnamon in a glass of water. Add a pinch of pepper powder and little honey. A tablespoon of the above concoction take 1/2 hour after meals relieves indigestion and flatulence (gas).
- Mix 1/4 teaspoon pepper powder, 1/4 teaspoon of cumin (jeera) powder to a glass of buttermilk. Have this 1-2 times a day.
- A golden rule to avoid indigestion; get up from the dining table when you can still eat some more or are a little hungry. Chew food well.

- Add 1 teaspoon fresh grated ginger (adrak) to 1 cup water. Cover and simmer on low heat for 5 minutes. Stain and drink 1-2 times a day.
- Soak one teaspoon of celery seeds in a glass of butter milk for 5-6 hours. Grind in the same buttermilk and drink it 1-2 times a day.
  - (*i*) Mix about 6gms. of castor oil with 20 gms of milk to clean the bowels.
  - (*ii*) Take roasted borax 3 gms. Bishop's seeds 3 gms, Kala Namak 3 gms, grind them to the powdered and pass through from the sieve or through a thick cloth. Administer 2 gms. of the powder everyday with lukewarm water.
- Mix 1 teaspoon mint juice, 1 teaspoon lemon juice, juice of 1/4 piece ginger and a pinch of black salt (kala namak) and drink it.
- Mix a little asafoetida (heeng) with water to make a paste. Apply on and around the navel.
- Drink 1-2 teaspoons brandy with a little warm water. Gives immediate relief from gas.
- Mix carom seeds (ajwain) with lemon juice and dry in the sun. Bottle it and have a teaspoon whenever you feel that sometheeng is wrong with your stomach (very good for stomach digestion, gas, indigestion etc.)
- And then there is the age old method of using a hot water bottle and lying down on your stomach to get relief.
- Swallow with warm water, 1 teaspoon carom seeds (ajwain) and pinch of salt.
- 1 teaspoon pure ghee mixed with a pinch of asafoetida (heeng), swallow with warm water.

INDIGESTION

- Take the seeds of tulsi and peepal in equal quantity and grind them to fine powder form. Now add 3 gms. of this

powder with a spoonful of honey and lick it twice a day to clear indigestion.
- Drinking the tea of tulsi leaves also brings quick relief. The filthy substance will get out of the body with sweat and urine. Alternatively add 1 gm. of rock salt in 10 gms. of tulsi leaves' paste and swallow it down with water.

STOMACH BURN

- Take 1 teaspoon fenugreek seeds (methi daana), powder along with milk or buttermilk twice daily for a few days.

STOMACH HEAVINESS

- Mix ¼ teaspoon powdered cumin (jeera) seeds and black pepper in a glass of buttermilk (chhach). Drink two or three times a day for 2-3 days.

ABDOMINAL PAIN

- Add ½ teaspoon camphor (kapoor) and 1 tablespoon sandalwood paste to 1 tablespoon warm mustard oil. Massage gently over the lower abdomen.

COLIC IN BABIES

- Boil a teaspoon of fennel seeds (saunf) in a cup of water. Boil for 2-3 minutes and keep it to cool for 15-20 minutes. Strain it. Add 1-2 teaspoon to every feed of milk of the baby. It helps cure colic.

CONSTIPATION

It can be caused by many reasons, the prime one being wrong eating habits of the person and wrong choice of food also. The following treatments are quite effective:
- Soak the powder of Amaltas 50gms. overnight and strain the water in the morning to drink it adding 20 gms. of sugar.

- Have a glass of water with a spoonful of honey added to it every night before you go to sleep.
- Take cumin seeds 20 gms; dry ginger 20 gms; white cumin seeds 20 gms; ammonium chloride 5gms; small cardamom 5 gms; bishop's seed (ajwain) 20 gms; pippli 10 gms; black pepper 10 gms., cloves 5 gms; asafoetida 5gms; Old jaggery 50gms; musk camphor 2 gms; grind and sieve all the ingredients after mixing together and keep the powder in a glass vessel. Then grind the powder again with the juice of ginger. Then grind it again with the juice of lemon. Add more lemon juice if dries up. grind the mixture well for 15 days and then dry it in shade. Dry it as much as to facilitate your making small balls out of the grind paste. For any stomach disorder have two of these tablets daily with water after meals to get rid of any stomach ailment.
- Take a glass of warm water with 1 teaspoon honey and juice of 1/2 a lemon, as first theeng in the morning.
- Soak 6-8 dates (khajoor) in a cup of water at night. Churn in the mixer in the morning & drink in the morning.
- Consume approx. 250-300gms. fresh grapes (angoor) everyday. When grapes are not in season, soak 12-15 raisins (kishmish) in water and have them. Raisins should be soaked for 24-48 hours and eaten early in the morning. The water in which they are soaked should also be drunk.
- Simply eat a few liquorice (mulathi) sticks. One of its many properties is that it is a natural laxative.

CONSTIPATION IN SMALL CHILDREN

- Whole wheat flour should be used and processed foods (maida, cheese, confectionery) should be avoided.

- Taking 2-3 teaspoons of isabgol in milk or warm water at bed time is very beneficial.
- Mix 1/2 teaspoon honey to 1/2-1 cup warm water and have it 2-3 times a day.
- Soak 6-8 raisins in hot water (depending on the age). When cool, crush well and strain. When given routinely even to little infants, it helps to regulate bowel movement (however care should be taken so as not to give too much otherwise the child might get loose motions).
- Consumption of 6-8 apricots(khumani) a day or 2-3 cucumbers (kheera) a day or 1-2 bananas a day is also very useful.
- Bulk forming vegetables like carrots, radish, spinach, cabbage or roughage creating theengs should be consumed. Instead of juice always opt for eating the fruit.
- The best way to treat this common problem is to have lots of fresh radish with black salt or rock-salt and lemon juice sprinkled on them. Radish is an ideal purgative. If one takes half a cup of fresh radish juice as the first theeng in the morning it is still better. Don't eat anytheeng till you have constipation. If possible have very light diet and eat radish as salad. If you have a little piece of jaggery over the radish diet, even the foul smell shall be considerably subsided.

LOOSE MOTIONS

When the system fails to digest the rich food, the body rejects it as it is in the form of the loose motion. Try the following treatments:

- Give about 5 gms. of Isabgol with cold water in which about 1 teaspoonful sugar has been added.
- Peel an apple and shred it. Keep the shredded pieces in a plate for approximately 20 minutes until they turn brown in colour and then eat them.
- Slice the tender unripe bel fruit. Sundry them. Powder the slices. Take 1 teaspoon along with warm water twice a day.
- Take every night. 3 cloves of garlic (lahsan), chopped and boiled in milk.
- Make a paste of 1 green chilli along with 2 tablespoon lime juice and 1/2 teaspoon camphor (kapoor). Take 1/4 teaspoon of this paste.
- 2 or 3 teaspoons coriander seeds (saboot dhania) soaked overnight in water and take next morning with 1 cup buttermilk (chhach).
- Boil 1/4 teaspoon powdered cardamom (chhoti illaichi) seeds in thin tea water and drink.
- Mix juice of 15-20 tender curry leaves (curry patta) with 1 teaspoon honey and drink.
- Apply ginger (adrak) juice around the navel.
- Combine 1 teaspoon each powdered ginger (adrak) powdered cumin (jeera) and powdered cinnamon (dalchini) with honey and make into a thick paste. Take 1 teaspoon thrice daily.
- Boil 1 teaspoon cumin seeds (jeera) in a glass of water. Add to this 1 teaspoon fresh juice of coriander leave (dhania) and a pinch of salt. Drink twice daily after meals for 2-3 days.

- Mash 1 ripe banana along with a pinch of salt and 1 teaspoon tamarind pulp (imli ka guda). Take twice a day.
- Drinking a unsweetened black tea is very effective for stopping diarrhoea.

For Children

- Ripe & sweet apples crushed to a pulp (can be steamed) can be given as 1-4 tablespoon several times a day.
- Mashed ripe banana with a little salt, should be taken 2-3 times a day.
- A teaspoon of date (khajoor) paste mixed with a little honey, given three times a day is very effective for regulating the bowels.
- 5-10 gms of amla seed powder mixed with buttermilk (chhach) should be taken for 1-2 days.
- Crush 8-10 curry leaves (curry patta). Mix with a cup of thin buttermilk (chhach) and have 2-3 times a day.
- Mix juice of 1 large pomegranate (anar) and 1 glass of sugarcane juice (ganne ka ras). Have 4 times a day.
- A fast with only buttermilk, curd and rice or bananas proves very effective.
- Avoid raw vegetables and fruits such as orange, sweet lime, papaya, pineapple and spices.
- Drink plenty of water to which a teaspoon of sugar and a pinch of salt has been added to guard against dehydration.
- A strong cup of unsweetened black tea is very effective.

Stools With Blood

- 1 tablespoon juice of the flower of pomegranate (anar) with sugar candy (mishri), taken twice daily.

DEHYDRATION

- Soak half a nutmeg (jaiphal) in 2 cups water for over 2-3 hours. Take 1 teaspoon of this infusion and mix in 1 cup fresh coconut water, drink thrice a day.

CHOLERA

This epidemic occurs in hot & humid season. It is invariably accompanied by frequent loose motions and loss of weight. If not treated in due time, this disease could be fatal. The remedies to check this disease are the following.

- Administer opium 5gms. in 10 gms. of edible lime to stop the loose motion.
- Grind the lemon seeds and mix it in rose water. Administer it orally for quick relief.
- Pull out the root of the plant swallow work(Aak in Hindi), clean the dirt from it and unpeel its rind. Add the black pepper with equal amount of this rind and form a paste of them. Then roll out small tablets. Administer each tablet with water at the interval of two hours.
- Take fresh mint leaves and grind them with small cardamoms. Boil both of them in water and thicken the fluid by heat. When the fluid is thick and homogeneous, let the patient sip it as and when he desires it. Take precaution to give lot of water to the patient to drink. Keep his clothes and beds clean. The affected patient must stay aloof.

FLATULENCE AND BELCHEENG

- Soak 3 tablespoons carom (ajwain) seeds in an adequate quantity of lime juice and dry in the shade. When fully dried, powder with a little black salt. Take 1 teaspoon of this mixture twice daily for a few days with a little warm water. (This treatment is more effective when fats and spices are avoided in the diet.)

- Grind 2 teaspoons each carom seeds and dried ginger into a fine powder. Add a little black salt. Take 1 teaspoon of this mixture with 1 cup warm water frequently.
- Powder together dry ginger with black pepper, equal amounts, say 1 teaspoon each and 3-4 cardamom (chooti illaichi) seeds. Have 1/2 teaspoon of this mixed with water to relieve gas.
- Apply a paste of asafoetida (heeng) mixed with water on the stomach.
- Make a coarse powder (churan) of equal amounts of cumin seeds (jeera), carom seeds (ajwain), black pepper corns (saboot kali mirch) and fenugreek seeds (methi daana). Have 1/2 teaspoon with water.
- To prevent gas from forming, chew a piece of fresh ginger after meals regularly.
- Add a teaspoon of caraway seeds to 1½-2 litres of water and boil it on low flame for 15 minutes. Strain and drink 1 cup of this tea, hot or warm 3 times a day after meals.
- A drop of dill oil (soye ka tel) mixed with a teaspoon of honey, licked immediately after meals is very effective in controlling gas.
- Wash black harad well with water and wipe with a clean dry cloth, store in a air tight bottle. Suck one piece after meals. Keep in the mouth till it dissolves completely. This is effective in controlling gas and constipation
- Mix ¼ teaspoon dry ginger powder (sonth) with a pinch of asafoetida (heeng) and a pinch of black salt (rock salt) (kala namak) in a little warm water and drink it.

- Mix 1-2 teaspoons brandy with warm water & drink for immediate relief from gas and stomach ache due to gas.
- Some people are allergic or have intolerance for milk, milk products and wheat products, but go through life without ever realizing this and keep suffering from acute gas trouble. Lactose intolerance (from milk) is being recognized in the west as also gluten intolerance (from wheat). Hence giving up these two theengs may greatly benefit you. Instead of wheat you can have rice or chapatis of maize, jawar or bajara.
- Take Bishop's seeds, 10 gms., dry ginger 6 gms., kala namak 3 gms., grind them well to powder form and administer thrice daily with water. Take 3 gms. of powder each time.
- Munch your food properly and eat slowly, without letting air enter your system when you gulp your food.'
- Take a spoonful of ginger juice, add salt and take it after your meals.
- Take dry ginger, Bishop's seeds, and about 2 spoonfuls of lemon juice. Mix them well and take the combination whenever you have a feeling of overfulness or any gastric trouble.
- Asaoetida should be an essential condiment of your food if you have this trouble. If you feel pain in your stomach, rub asafoetida added to water over and around your navel.

Hiccups

- Grind 4 cardamom(chhoti illaichi) well. Boil it in 2½ cups or ½ litre water. When about 1 cup water remains, remove from fire and sieve it through a muslin cloth. Let it cool. When warm, drink a glassful. It works like magic.

Disorders of Digestive System 87

- Suck 2-3 small pieces of fresh ginger (adrak). This helps in hiccups which keep occurring again and again.
- Drink ½ glass water, slowly.
- Keep a teaspoon of sugar in your mouth and suck slowly.
- Swallow ½ teaspoon mustard seeds mixed with ½ teaspoon pure ghee.
- Take five gms. of turmeric and five gms. of Urad pulse. Grind them to fine powder, put them in a live chilum and take a long puff. The hiccups trouble will be instantly cured.

NAUSEA & VOMITING

- Mix ½ teaspoon of fresh ginger (adrak) juice with 1 teaspoon each of fresh lime, mint (pudina) juice and 1 tablespoon of honey and drink.
- Slice a ripe banana, sprinkle some powdered sugar and freshly grind cardamoms (chhoti illaichi) on top. Eat 1-2 times a day.
- Eat ½ teaspoon grind cumin seeds (jeera).
- Ginger (adrak) tea or sucking sliced ginger (adrak) work by interrupting nausea signals sent from the stomach to the brain. If you are a herbal tea drinker simply sprinkle powdered cinnamon on the tea and drink. To make ginger tea, simply simmer a few slices of ginger in hot tea water.

VOMITING DUE TO INDIGESTION

- Frequent intake of lime juice is a good remedy.
- Licking the powder of fried cloves (laung) mixed with honey controls vomiting.
- Sucking a piece of ice also controls vomiting.
- Mix 2-3 teaspoon of curry leaves (curry patta) juice with a teaspoon of lime juice (can add little sugar if needed) .

Drinking this will control morning sickness, nausea and vomiting.

- Crush 2-3 cloves of garlic (lahsan) and boiled with 3/4 cup of water or milk. Boil till half the amount remains and then drink. It takes care of all digestive disorders.

WORMS IN STOMACH & INTESTINES

- If you have only carrot or preparation made of carrot for a few days, the worms shall vanish. The best course is to have enough of jalebi and milk combination followed by carrot pickle soaked in mustard seeds water. This treatment will centralise the wormround jalebi - milk combination and the mustard water soaked carrot would kill them and expel them out of the system.
- The smell of radish is enough to drive away even the poisonous insects let alone these worms. Just have radish juice mixed with rock salt and lemon juice twice a day, preferably after every meal. In less than three days you would find your intestines are clear of these worms. In fact, having a little of this juice after every meal is an ideal way to prevent the occurrence of these worms.
- Fry fenugreek seeds in a little ghee & grind to a powder. Store in an airtight bottle. Add some powder to drinking water and drink 2-3times daily for 2-3 days.
- Take 1 tablespoon juice extracted from bitter gourd (karela) leaves. Mix into a glassful of buttermilk and take every morning.
- Steep some cloves (laung) in ½ cup water for 6 to 8 hours and use it for enema.

- Fry 1 teaspoon dried neem flowers in 1 teaspoon ghee and mix with 1 cup boiled rice and eat twice or thrice a day.

- Slice and dry the kernel of mango. Mix 1 tablespoon fenugreek seeds (methi daana) and powder it. Take 1 teaspoon in buttermilk.

- Eat papayas frequently.

- Take 5-10 seeds of bitter gourd (karela) and crush them. Fry them in a little ghee. Take twice daily.

- Soak mustard seeds overnight or for two days and when the water turns sour give it to the patient after meals.

- Ask the patient to eat a ripe and roasted-on fire tomato as the first theeng in the morning for three to four days.

- Take 25 gms. of the rind of the roots of pomegranate plant and three times boil it. When water remains half of the original quantity, strain the water and divide into three dosages. Have first dose in the morning as the first theeng and the other doses after two hourly interval. Have about 10 gms. of castor oil after the last dose. Your worms in the stomach will clear out.

HAEMORRHOIDS (PILES)

Piles or haemorrhoids, is a varicose and often inflamed condition of the veins about the lower end of the bowel. The piles are either external or internal or mixed. In external piles there is not much bleeding but a lot of pain, whereas the internal piles consist in discharge of several ounces of dark blood through anus. Try the following treatments:

- Radish is an ideal antidote for this disorder. Take a cupful of radish juice and add about 5gms. of pure ghee. Mix them well with a spoon and drink this potion in the evening and in the morning.
- Take a long radish & divide in four equal parts lengthwise. Apply a little of salt and keep it in the open for the entire night so that fresh dew may fall over it. Have it as the first theeng in the morning. After passing stool, wash the anus with radish water.
- If piles are bleeding type, have masoor dal in your lunch, followed by sour but fresh whey.
- Take the kernel of Bakain seeds about 20gms., add 6 gms of black pepper and knead them together to form tiny tablets. Have 3 gms. of the tablets in the morning and 3gms. in the evening after mixing Khand sugar into it.
- These troubles include many ailments including enlargement of liver, bitter belches, wind trouble and the like. The main cause could be congenital, due to wrong habits or as a symptom to some other functional disturbance in the body. Try the following treatments:
- Eat radish as much as you can with your meals or afterwards. Sugarcane juice should be an essential part of your diet.
- Take two gms. of the pith of Amaltas, hari makoya', grind them to paste form and apply it over your live region.
- Always piss while standing after your principal meals whether you feel the urge or not. Try to sleep on your leftside after your principal meals. Just take five grams of turmeric powder mixed in a glassful of separated Mattha (whey) every morning and evening to reactivate the sluggish liver and repair the damage.

- Take 5 tulsi leaves, 2 gms., roasted powder of cumin seeds and 2 gms. of black salt. Grind them together to make it in a homogeneous powder form. Add to it even amount of the kernel of the wood apple. Mix the combination in about 100 gms. of curd to reactivate the sluggish liver. For early relief from any sort of stomach disorder, drink a spoonful of the combination of the juices of tulsi and ginger.

FISTULA

- Have three or four tulsi leaves every morning with water or put them in your water are likely to drink at least half an hour before you actually imbibing it. Alternatively take the root of tulsi plant and the fruit of neem tree (Nimboli) and grind them together. Take 2 gms. of this combination every morning with whey for quick relief.

JAUNDICE

- Twenty grams of leaves of heena should be steeped in water overnight, The mixture should be strained in the morning and drink for a few days. Juice of leaves of Horse Radish should be boiled and strained. Twenty grams of raw sugar should be added to the mixture and drink. The yellow pigment in the eyes can be dealt effectively by grinding seven grains of small fennel in a women's milk and introduced into the nostrils.
- A fine paste of tender papaya leaves, about 1/2 teaspoon paste, is taken with some water.
- Pour over a handful of lime leaves in 1 cup hot water and take the infusion.

- Make a fine powder of 1 teaspoon each crushed liquorice root, chicory seeds (kaasni) and rock salt (kala namak). Take ½ teaspoon with water twice daily.
- 1 to 2 teaspoon fresh juice of coriander (dhania) leaves is mixed in 1 cup buttermilk and taken 2-3 times.
- Mash a ripe banana along with 1 tablespoon honey and eat twice a day for a few days.
- Frequently take lime juice.
- Take ¼ teaspoon turmeric (haldi) along with a glass of hot water 2 or 3 times daily.
- ½ teaspoon ginger juice with 1 teaspoon each fresh lime and mint juice mixed with a tablespoon of honey. Take it frequently.
- Finely grind some bel leaves. Take 1 teaspoon of this paste along with a pinch of black pepper and follow it with 1 cup of butter milk thrice a day.

Yellow Pigmentation in Eyes due to Jaundice

- Grind ¼ teaspoon black cumin seeds (kala jeera) in breast milk and introduce a pinch into the nostrils.
- The main theeng to be remembered in a case of jaundice is that if the liver is not burdened (through daily flusheeng of the intestines) and a fat free diet is taken, the organ will recover its vitality even without medication. Sweet substances and liquids like sugarcane juice, fruit juices and dry grapes should form the mainstay of a patient's diet. About 100 grams of dried Tamarind (Imali) pith should be soaked in water overnight together with half the quantity of dried plums (alloo bhukhara), mashed and the thick

liquid taken by adding a little black salt to it in the morning. The patient should take as much whey as he can during the day.
- Add 10 gms. tulsi leaves' juice in about 50gms. of radish juice. Add a little of jaggery to the combination to sweeten it. Have this solution twice or thrice daily for about a month for getting total relief from this problem.
- Alternatively take 3 gms. of tulsi leaves' juice and 3 gms. of the root of punarnava. Mix them both in 50 gms. of water and drink it for about 15 days. This is a very effective dose to cure jaundice.

FLATULENCE

- Take about 10 gms. of tulsi juice, 10 gms. of dry ginger and 20 gms. of jaggery. Mix all of them together to form small tablets. Take this tablet thrice a day with water to set right your digestive process. But during the period you have this trouble, better keep fast or take only easily digestible food.

PILES

- Wash 2-3 dried figs (anjeer) very well & soak in a glass of cold water overnight. Have it first theeng in the morning. Have them for 2-3 weeks for good results. It is effective in ordinary as well as bleeding piles.
- 3 teaspoon of the juice of the leaves of bittergourd mixed with a glassful of buttermilk taken every morning for a month is a good remedy for piles.

- The juice of radish (Mooli) or consuming fresh radish is very effective. The juice should be given in dose of 60-90 ml, morning & evening.
- Take 1/2 teaspoon each of powder of dried pomegranate flowers, poppy seeds & dried neem leaves, twice a day with milk for bleeding piles.
- Mix juice of 15-20 tender curry leaves (curry patta) with 1 teaspoon honey & drink.
- Take 1 tablespoon black cumin seeds and roast them. Mix in another tablespoon of black cumin seeds and powder them finely. Take 1/2 teaspoon of this powder with a glass of water everyday.

APPETITE LOSS (ANOREXIA)

- Take 2 teaspoons of amla juice and mix it with 2 teaspoon honey and 2 teaspoons lime juice. Add 1 cup water and drink on an empty stomach every morning. To take out juice from fresh amla, remove seeds from fresh amla and grind the pulp into a fine paste. Tie it in a muslin cloth and squeeze out the juice. Whenever fresh fruits are not available take dried amla at night in a cup of water, strain it the next morning. Add 1/8 teaspoon black pepper powder (kali mirch) and 2 teaspoon lime juice. Dilute it if necessary with water and drink every morning regularly on an empty stomach.
- Take ½ teaspoon black pepper powder (kali mirch) and 1 tablespoon jaggery powder (shakkar) mixed together.
- Mix half teaspoon each of carom seeds (ajwain), fennel seeds (saunf), dried ginger powder (sonth), salt and black

cumin seeds (shah jeera). Swallow about 3/4 teaspoon of this mixture with water 2-3 times a day.

Dehydration

- Add 1/4 teaspoon salt, 3 teaspoon brown sugar or ordinary sugar and 2 teaspoon lime juice to 1 cup of water, mix well and drink.

Disorders of Muscles and Joints

In our daily life, we suffer from sprain, backache and body aches. Here are the remedies for various muscular & joint disorders:-

Muscular Cramps

- Apply clove oil on the affected parts.

Sprain

- Chop raw onions and put in a towel. Place this over the sprain to relieve pain and bring down the swelling. Alternatively, make a footbath of lavender oil and water and soak your ankle, but do not massage the area.
- Grind lime leaves into a fine paste. Mix it with an equal quantity of butter. Apply on the affected areas.
- Mix equal parts of almonds oil & garlic oil and massage over the affected parts.
- Take 1 gram flour, just a pinchful, and add half of its quantity with equal amount of turmeric powder. Add linseed oil in it or any other oil like of mustard or til, and make the poultice . Apply it on the sprained portion. The poultice will enhance the blood circulation and in two days' time the relief will be there.

Disorders of Muscles and Joints

Muscular Pain

- Warm the papaya leaf over the fire and apply on affected parts.
- Heat ginger (adrak) paste with turmeric (haldi) paste (1:1) and apply.
- Soak ½ teaspoon liquoric (mulathi) root powder in 1 cup water and leave overnight. Mix into the infusion 1 cup rice gruel (cooked broken rice) and take every morning.

Rib Pain

- Grind a turmeric piece and mix in a hot water to form a thick paste. Apply this paste over the ribs acheeng. Soon the pain will vanish. In case you feel you are not having the desired effect, prepare the oil of turmeric and lightly massage your acheeng ribs with this oil. Another treatment for quick relief is to mix turmeric powder in the milk of the Aak plant (the medicinal plant, swallow worf, whose botanical name is Calotropes Gigantea) and apply over the ribs. This paste will quickly give relief.

Ankle Swelling & Pain

- Mix equal quantities of castor oil and lime juice. Massage the affected area with the mixture. Also drink 1 cup warm water mixed with lime juice and honey.

Heels Having Pain

- Mix equal amounts by weight of carom seeds (ajwain) onion seeds (kalaunji), fenugreek seeds (methi daana) and saboot isabgol. Have 1 tablespoon everyday first theeng in the morning. If you can grind them slightly in the mixer- makes it more effective. This treatment takes a couple of months but is a sure shot remedy.

Note: Saboot isabgol, tiny very light pinkish particles, will be available with your grocer or if you request him he will get it for you from the wholesale market. Do not use the husk which is generally used by people for constipation as that is less effective but not harmful. If saboot isabgol is not available, husk can be used. It takes longer for the pain to go.

LEGS, SWELLING AND PAIN

- Mix equal quantities of castor oil and lime juice. Massage the affected area with this mixture. Also drink 1 cup warm water mixed with lime juice and honey.

ATHLETES'S FOOT

Keeping your feet clean and dry is enough to discourage the growth of this fungal infection. Remember, it is infectious and you must keep and wash your shoes, socks, and towel separately. To sooth the broken areas of your feet, simply soak them for 10 minutes in a foot-both of apple cider vinegar mixed with water.

FOOT CORNS

- Tie a fresh slice of lemon over the corn (painful area) and keep it all night.
- Massage castor oil on the corns every morning and night before sleeping.
- Massage for 2-3 minutes so that the oil gets absorbed. In 3-4 weeks the corns will disappear.
- Mash 1-2 cloves (laung) & garlic (lahsan) and tie over the corns. Keep overnight.

SCIATICA

- Take just 10 gms. of turmeric and grind it in 100 gms. of cow's urine. Add about 25 gms. of castor oil to it and

Disorders of Muscles and Joints

make the patient drink the whole lot. The patient will get relief. Alternatively make the patient inhale deeply the vapours emerging out of the large vessel in which jaggery is being prepared from the sugarcane juice. But the patient must keep his body covered with a heavy blanket. The more he sweats, the quicker he will be cured.

Paralysis

- Boil a few leaves of tulsi in a tumbler full of water. When cool, strain and put this water in a bottle. Massage this water on the affected limbs. Continue this treatment for at least two weeks. This treatment, coupled with regular intake of the tulsi leaves as an alternative treatment along with other remedies is helpful in giving good results.

Fainting

- A hot poultice of carom seeds (ajwain) may be used as dry fomentation for hands and feet.

Fatigue

- Take a glass of grapefruit and lemon juice in equal parts to dispel fatigue and general tiredness after a days' work.

Body Weakness

- Soak 8 to 10 almonds and 1 teaspoon rice overnight. Remove the outer skin of almonds. Grind into a fine paste. Mix in some milk and pinch of turmeric powder (haldi). Boil and drink along with sugar candy (mishri) or ordinary sugar to taste.
- Sprinkle the following on a platter of mango slices; 1 teaspoon honey, a pinch of saffron (kesar), cardamom (chhoti illaichi) and rose water (gulab jal). Take twice daily.

Exhaustion due to Overwork

- Boil ¼ teaspoon powdered cardamom (chhoti illaichi) seeds in thin tea water and drink.

Gout-Swelling

- Take 250 gms. of turmeric powder, 50 gms; Kuchala powder, 50gms; pigeon dung, 100 gms; castor oil and 250gms. til oil. Mix both the oils, add turmeric, kuchala and pigeons dung and boil. When the solid contents turn black, cool and strain the oil mixture. Add to it a cup of kerosene oil. Repeatedly massage this oil on your joints. Always massage the adjoining areas before massaging the swollen part. Like if you have to massage your knees, first massage the upper thigh and thigh joint before massaging the knees. This way the raw phlegm will be dissolved and not shifted to other portion. Try not to have constipation when you take this massage course.

Gouty Pains

- Mix mustard oil and rectified alcohol (1 part of oil to 40 parts alcohol) and use as a lotion.
- Make a poultice of ground fenugreek seeds (methi dana) use on the affected part.
- Equal quantities of Asparagus seeds (halong). Black cumin, fenugreek (methi) and Ajwain should be taken and swallowed every morning in dose of 3 grams. The remedies are also recommended for rheumatism and lumbago.

Rheumatism

- Heat the leaves of the plant swallow worf (Aak in Hindi) and tie them over the affected joints.
- Grind the guava leaves to a paste form and apply on the affected joint.

- Take about 750 gms. of the root of Arand plant and boil it in 6 kgs. of water. When it is reduced to 1/4th of its normal quantity, then add castor oil to it and boil again till whole of the water in the mixture evaporates leaving only the oily substance. Strain this oil through a fine muslin cloth and keep it preserved, in a glass bottle. Massage your limbs with this oil at least 15mts. before you go to have your bath. In case you do it after your bath, then tie cotton wads after the massage over the affected joints.
- Take 'Binaules', cut, grind and sieve them and boil in water, when only thick paste remains. Dry it and then tie it over your affected joints.

Rheumatic Pain

- Boil 3 tablespoon powdered nutmeg (jaiphal) in 1 cup sesame oil (til ka tel). Cool and apply on affected parts.
- 2 to 3 teaspoon pepper powder is fried in 2 teaspoons sesame oil (til ka tel) until charred. When it is warm, it is applied on the affected areas and massaged lightly.
- A 3 inch piece of dried ginger is grinded with a grape sized piece of asafoetida (heeng) in milk. The paste is applied on the affected area. The area is exposed to the sun for imparting warmth and heat.
- The patient must avoid fried eatables and sour foods like curds and alcohol, moong dal, meat soup, garlic, onions, bitter gourd, papaya and green bananas are the foods which help in controlling gout and rheumatic pain.

Joint Pain

- Take equal quantities of asparagus seeds (shatavari), black cumin seeds (shah jeera), fenugreek (methi daana) seeds and carom seeds (ajwain). Powder and take 1/2 teaspoon every morning.

- Combine 6 teaspoons each of ginger (adrak) and caraway seeds along with 3 teaspoons of black pepper corns (saboot kali mirch) and grind into a fine powder. Have ½ teaspoon with water twice daily.
- Soak 1-2 teaspoons fenugreek seeds (methi daana) in a cup of curd overnight. Eat in the morning on an empty stomach or soak 1-2 teaspoons fenugreek seeds (methi daana) in 1 cup water overnight. Drink the water first theeng in the morning and also eat the methi seeds.
- Take out 1 tablespoon juice of fresh leaves of bathua and drink every day on an empty stomach for 2-3 months. Do not add anytheeng to the juice and do not eat anytheeng before and after, for 2 hours.
- Make a tea from papaya seeds and have 6-7 cups a day, for at least 2 weeks.
- Have 1-2 garlic (lahsan) cloves or 1 garlic, which has only 1 clove in a pod, first theeng in the morning.
- Mix 1 teaspoon of dry amla powder with 2 teaspoons of jaggery (gur) and have it twice daily for a month.

ARTHRITIS

Extract the juice of carrots and add to it the juice of Karnphool (Dandelion). Have just 5 gms. of carrot juice and add only half of the quantity the juice of dandelion. Drink this combination regularly for at least 15 days for speedier relief. It is also advisable to rub Mahanarayani oil on the joints.

BED SORES

- Apply honey on the length and breadth of a banana leave and lie on it for a few hours. Ensure its contact with the affected parts.

Disorders of Muscles and Joints

Body Pain
- Boil 3 tablespoons powdered nutmeg (jaiphal) in 1 cup sesame oil (til ka tel), cool it and apply on affected parts.

Body Swelling
- Grind black cumin seeds (shah jeera) with a little hot water and apply on affected parts.

Body and Muscles Development
- Soak 2 almonds, 5 pista kernels and 1 teaspoon poppy seeds in 1 cup cow's milk for an hour. Grind it and add some more warm milk. Take daily for 3 months.

Bruises
- Slice a raw onion & place over the bruises. Do not apply this to broken skin.

13

Skin and Hair Problems

Skin is not only the outer covering of the body but it is a sense an excretary organ also. The glow of skin shows our good health.

SKIN CRACKED

- For dry, cracked hands apply a mixture of grated potato soaked in olive oil. Leave this on for 10 minutes and then rinse off.

FOR FACE

Pound a piece of radish to a pulp and just apply this pulp on the face. Keep it till it is dry. Then rub it off by cold water. Internally, consume radish, its juice and the radish vegetable cooked by steam heat. It is better to leave salt altogether till your blood is clean. The acne results because of impurity of blood.

- Mix 1 teaspoon lemon juice in 1 teaspoon finely grind cinnamon (dalchini) powder and apply on affected areas frequently. Sift the cinnamon (dalchini) powder to make it into a very fine powder.
- Crush a few garlic (lahsan) flakes and apply on the face, once or twice a day. Swallowing 1-2 flakes of raw garlic regularly helps further.

Skin and Hair Problems

- Grind some neem leaves with water to a fine paste. Apply on infected area.
- Make a paste of 1/2 teaspoon each of sandalwood and turmeric (haldi) powder in little water and apply.
- Grind some black cumin seeds (Jeera) with a little vinegar (sirka) to a smooth paste. Apply on affected parts.
- Clean face with cotton wool dipped in rose water 2-3 times a day. Do not use soap.
- Orange peel is very good in the treatment of acne. Grind the peel with some water to a paste and apply on affected parts. When oranges are not in season, you may use a powder of dried orange peels. For this, when oranges are in season, dry orange peels in shade. Powder finely in a grinder and sift it to make it a very fine powder. Store in an air tight bottle for future use.

BLACKHEADS

- Mix 1 teaspoon lime juice in 1 teaspoon finely grind cinnamon (dalchini) powder and apply on affected areas frequently.
- Mix 1 teaspoon each turmeric (haldi) powder and juice of fresh coriander (dhania) leaves and apply daily as a face before going to sleep.

PIMPLES

- Grind equal quantity of nutmeg (jaiphal), black pepper (kali mirch) and sandalwood. Apply on affected area.
- Clean face with rose water (gulab) 2-3 times a day.
- The orange peel (santre ka chilka) is very valuable in the treatment of acne & pimples. Pound the peel with water on a piece of stone and apply on the affected area. When

oranges are not in season, dry peels in the shade. Powder the dried peels. Sift to get a fine powder & store.
- Rub nutmeg (jaiphal) in unboiled milk to form a paste. Apply on the face & let it dry. Wash it off with warm water. Do it 2-3 times a day. You will see the pimples disappearing in 3-4 days.
- A couple of garlic (lahsan) cloves crushed & rubbed on the face 1-2 times a day. This process is further helped by taking raw garlic regularly. Have 1-2 cloves in the morning.
- Apply fresh lemon juice on the affected area overnight. Wash off with warm water next morning.
- Grind some neem leaves with water to a fine paste. Apply on infected area
- Application of fresh mint (pudina) juice over face every night cures pimples and prevents dryness of the skin.
- Mix equal amounts of lemon juice and rose water (gulab jal). Apply on face and keep for ½ an hour. 15-20 days of this application helps cure pimples and also removes blemishes & scars.

SCARS ON FACE

- Wash face with coconut water (nariyal pani). Apply coconut water on face and leave for 15-20 minutes before washeeng it off.
- Grind one teaspoon yellow mustard (peeli rai) to a paste with 1 tablespoon malai/cream & apply on face and neck. Leave for 15-20 minutes. This also removes itcheeng as well as blemishes from the skin.
- Wash & grind a few fresh mint (pudina) leaves to a smooth paste. Apply & leave for half an hour or apply every night before going to sleep. This helps in getting rid of pimples along with the blemishes.

- Apply a teaspoon of olive oil mixed with 1/2 teaspoon of lime juice, leave it for 20-25 minutes & then wash off.
- Take the pulp of a ripe tomato. Add a few drops of lemon juice & rub on the face and neck. Leave for 20-25 minutes before washeeng.
- If your skin is dry, rub a stick of sandalwood in milk & if skin is oily, rub it in rose water (gulab jal) and then apply on face. Leave for an hour and then wash with cold water. This is very effective during summers.
- For a dry & blemished skin, mix a tablespoon gram flour (besan), add a pinch of turmeric (haldi), 1/4 teaspoon orange peel(or santre ka chilka) powder, a teaspoon curd (dahi) & a teaspoon of milk. Apply on face & neck. When skin feels taunt, rub it off with finger tips, and wash off with tap water.

SCARS DUE TO BURN

- Boil 1 cup neem bark in 4 cups water. Remove from fire and shake liquid. Apply the emerging froth on the affected area. Repeat several times and for several days.
- Peel & grind a few almonds to a fine paste with 2 tablespoons milk and one tablespoon each of orange & carrot juice. Apply well on the face and neck. Leave for half an hour, then wash off.
- Apply one tablespoon finely grind raw papaya on face and neck. Keep for 15-20 minutes and wash off.

PUSTULES

- Take half kg turmeric powder and boil it and add about 200 gms. of pure honey to it. Keep the mixture as it is for two weeks in a glass jar. Now strain it and fill in a clean bottle. Take 10 to 15 gms. of this Aasav (mixture) after food. This will cleanse your blood of the impurities which cause pustules. Also dip a cotton piece in turmeric oil and place it over pustules for relief.

To Open Shrinked Pores Of The Skin

- Mix one tablespoon tomato juice and a few drops of lemon juice. Apply on open pores. Wash after 15-20 minutes.
- Rub a cube of ice everyday, on the area where open pores are present. Wash face with cold water. Never use hot water on face.

Face - Freckles (Jhanyin)

- These are mainly caused by using creams and lotions indiscriminately which burn the outer layer of the skin. Take just 10 gms. of grind turmeric and drench it in the milk of the banyan, peepal or aak tree. Make a thick and uniform paste of it in the evening and cover it with a lid. Keep it as it is overnight. Massage your face with this ubtan at least half an hour before you take your bath. Continue this treatment for a week to remove all the freckles. Then use ubtan just once a week.

The decoction or Karha

- Decoction made out of chukander or beetroot leaves is very effective to cure this trouble. You can prepare the karha in the following manner:
- Take a few pieces of beetroot (chukander) and dice them to small pieces. Boil them in water when they become tender, crush them as much as to reduce them to a pulp. Again add a little water and boil the whole lot once again. When you find the solution becoming homogeneous and thick, cool it and strain it through a coarse cloth or strainer. The karha is ready. Wash your hands and feet with this karha everyday when you retire for the day. It is always

better to keep your hands and feet immersed in this diluted karha before washeeng them with the water. In about a couple of days your skin will become soft and glowing. This karha would be used for application on the dry face.

Skin Allergies

- Grind 1 tablespoon poppy seeds (khuskhus) with 1 teaspoon water. Add 1 teaspoon lime juice. Apply on the affected areas.
- Mix 1 teaspoon lime juice with sandalwood paste and apply all over.

Skin Irritation

- Take clean water and rub vigorously a piece of cucumber to make its thick paste. Then apply the paste on the skin for its cure in two three days time. But the patient should not consume heat producing items like spicy food, tea and even lots of common salt.

Itcheeng

- Extract juice of tulsi and massage on the parts of the body itcheeng. If the trouble be chronic, take about 2 parts of tulsi juice and one part of til oil. Allow them to boil on slow fire. Then cool it and put it in a bottle. This is most effective oil for all sorts of itcheeng problems.

Ring worms

- Take a large piece of pure turmeric and gently rub it over a stone slab (sil) drenched with water. Take out the rubbed portion of turmeric from the stone slab and apply the paste over the rings on your body. When the paste dries apply another layer of the turmeric paste over it. In a couple of days time the trouble will start to end and the sprouts will also disappear. Don't discontinue the treatment once you get well. It is better to apply the paste for a week more for total relief.

Eczema

- Add 1 teaspoon camphor (kapoor) to 1 teaspoon sandalwood paste and apply on the affected areas.
- Mix a paste of turmeric (haldi) and neem leaves (1:1) in a little gingelly oil (til ka tel) and apply on affected areas.
- Grind 1 tablespoon each turmeric (haldi), neem leaves and gingelly oil (til ka tel) into a fine paste and apply on the affected parts.
- Rub a nutmeg (jaiphal) against a smooth stone slab with a little water and make a paste. Apply on affected parts.
- Stop using any soap and wash your body with neem soap.
- Grind pure sulphur and add in pure mustard oil and apply on your body.
- Take about 6 gms. of soda bicarb and pour in the juice of half a lemon over it. Add about 20 gms. of mustard oil and massage your body vigorously with this mixture. Then take sun-bath for about 2 hours before you go to take your bath. It is especially effective if your skin is dry.
- Extract the juice of leaves of beetroot and mixing it with honey, Apply it over the affected part. In about a week's time this trouble will end.
- apply freshly pounded radish pulp over the affected part. Allow it to dry. In about half an hour take bath in hot water in which some perfume is added. In about a week's treatment the affliction shall be removed.

Warts

- Mash the garlic (lahsan) cloves and apply externally.

Skin and Hair Problems

- Apply the milky juice coming out from the stems of figs (anjeer) and leaves on the affected areas.
- Place some chopped onions in a dish. Cover with salt and leave overnight. Twice a day apply the resulting juice to the warts until they disappear.
- Another alternative is fresh pineapple juice or slices. Since pineapple contains an enzyme that breaks down warts, it is very effective in removing warts without leaving behind any marks. Apply some to the warts several times in a day until it has gone.

SUNBURN

- Mix 2 teaspoons tomato juice and 4 tablespoons buttermilk (chhach). Apply it. Wash after 1/2 an hour.
- Mix olive oil with equal quantity of vinegar and apply an hour before your bath.

SWEATING EXCESSIVE

- Mix dry sandalwood powder in rose water (gulab jal) (1:1) and apply over parts where sweating is excessive.

THORN

- If a thorn has gone in your child's foot and is not coming out, simply mix jaggery (gur) and carom seeds (ajwain) and tie on it. The thorn will come out on it's own.

WRINKLES

- Apply coconut oil on the portions of skin and face where wrinkles set in and gently massage every night at bed time.
- Soak shredded ginger (adrak) in honey. Eat a spoonful every morning.

Body Dry Itch

- Grind 1 tablespoon poppy seeds (khuskhus) with 1 teaspoon water. Add 1 teaspoon lime juice. Apply on the affected areas.

Body Heat

- Add 2 to 3 drops of almond oil to pomegranate (anaar) juice and drink.
- Remove seeds from fresh amla fruits and grind the pulp into a fine paste. Tie it in a muslin cloth and squeeze out the juice. Take 2 teaspoons of this juice and mix it with two teaspoonfuls each honey and lime juice. Add 1 cup water and drink on an empty stomach every morning.
- Take a tender bel fruit. Grind it with 1 cup milk. Apply on the head and massage well before taking a shower.
- Soak 8 to 10 almonds and 1 teaspoon rice overnight. Remove the outer skin. Grind into a fine paste. Mix with some milk and add a pinch of turmeric powder (haldi) and sugar candy (mishri) to taste. Boil and drink.

Burns By Fire

- Immediately apply glycerine on the burnt area.
- Burn a handful of mango leaves to ashes and apply this on the affected parts.

Burns By Hot Water

- Take the thin bugs of banana leaves. Bandage directly on affected areas. Tie the upper part for two days and then lower parts for two more days.

Skin and Hair Problems

Palms, Burning Sensation

- Grind a handful of bitter gourd (karela) leaves into a smooth paste and apply on the affected areas of feet and palms frequently.
- Finely grind a handful of henna (mehendi) leaves and add 2 tablespoon lime juice. Stir and apply on the feet.
- Apply finely grated bottle gourd (lauki) on the feet.
- Mash 1 ripe banana along with a little curd and water, take twice a day.
- Grind a handful of bitter gourd (karela) leaves into a smooth paste and apply on the affected areas of feet and palms frequently.

Heat Exhaustion

- Apply some sandalwood oil on the forehead.

Heat Stroke

- Have the cooling drink 'panna'. To prepare this, cook unripe or green mangoes in hot ashes. Extract the pulp and mix with water and sugar. You may even pressure cook the mangoes if you cannot make provision for the ashes.

Prickly Heat

- Mix dry sandalwood powder with rose water (Gulab jal) to make a paste. Apply on affected parts. When dry, wash it off. If prevents excessive sweating & heals inflammed skin.

Burns, Scar

- Boil 1 cup neem bark (neem ki khal) in 4 cups water. Remove from fire and shake liquid. Apply the emerging froth on the affected area. Repeat several times and for several days.

Burns on Body

- Apply curry leaves (kari patta) as poultices over affected areas.
- Spread a thin layer of honey over the burn and cover with a dressing. Repeat this regularly every two or three hours till it heals.
- Mash a ripe banana and apply on burns. Bandage with betel leaves (pan ka patta).
- If you have a minor burn, immediately place an ice pack on the burnt area for 10 minutes.
- Combine 4 teaspoons each of lime juice coconut oil and rub until the mixture turns white. Apply on affected parts.

Cracked Feet/Soles

- Finely grind a handful of heena (mehendi) leaves. Add 2 tablespoons lemon juice and apply on the feet.
- Mix the juice of bottle gourd (lauki) and sesame oil (til ka tel) in the ratio 4:1 and heat till the moisture has evaporated. Bottle and use over cracked skin.
- Mix equal quantities of glycerine and lemon juice. Apply every night before going to bed. This mixture can be made and stored in a glass bottle.
- Massage your feet with castor oil every night (in winters) for 2-3 minutes and then wear socks at night.
- Grind equal amounts of neem leaves & turmeric (haldi). Apply on affected area.

Feet Smelling Bad

- Soak feet in strong tea for 20 minutes everyday until the smell disappears. To prepare your footbath, dip two tea bags in 500 ml of water for 15 minute and pour the tea into a basin containing two litres (10 cups) of cool water.

Unpleasant Body Odour

- Soak 10-15 basil leaves in 1 cup water and eat every morning for a month.

Grind neem (azadiracta indica) leaves and apply in armpits & on other parts of body.

Black Spots

- These may be caused by excessive indulgence in the sexual pleasures which sap your vitality and these black spots appear. Extract a little juice of tulsi and add two times more lime juice. Make their homogeneous solution and apply this solution or paste over these spots every night with soft hands. The spots will be removed in a week's time.

Boils

- Slightly roast big onion on a naked flame. Mash it and mix in a teaspoon each turmeric powder and ghee. Apply and tie a bandage.
- Mash the garlic (lahsan) cloves and apply externally.
- Grind neem leaves into a paste and apply on affected parts.
- Apply a paste of ginger (adrak) powder and turmeric (haldi) 1:1) on boils.
- Grind some black cumin seeds (kala jeera) in a little water and apply the paste on the affected areas.
- Heat black pepper powder in 1/2 teaspoon ghee until charred. Use this as an ointment.
- Take fenugreek leaf (methi patta) paste, heat it and when lukewarm, apply on the affected part of the body.
- Soak bread in warm milk and sandwich the mixture in between the folds of a clean cotton cloth. Apply this poultice to the boil and hold in place with a cotton

bandage. This draws the dirt to the surface of the skin and simultaneously bursts the boil.

Hair Falling

- Take a handful of neem leaves and boil them in 2 cups of water. After cooling and filtering, use the decoction for rinsing hair.

Baldness

- Collect the soft and green leaves of beetroot and boil a few in water. When the leaves become tender and soft take them out of the water. Now grind the leaves fully to a homogeneous pulp. If water is needed, only that water should be used in which the leaves had been boiled.
- Repeat the procedure in a similar way but this time replacing the beetroot leaves with henna. Now grind both the leaves together. Apply this paste over the head liberally. Allow it to dry and then wash it with lukewarm water in which a few drops of lime juice have been added. Repeat the process for one full month. It is expected that within this period hair will again start to sprout on the bald area. After doing this treatment for one full month, repeat it after every week. It is a very good remedy and many bald people have now lush growth of hair. But, as told earlier, it could be useful only when the baldness has not been due to the hereditary factor.
- Rub on the scalp 1 teaspoon oil in which raw mangoes have been preserved for over one year. Repeat this treatment frequently.
- Grind 1 tablespoon liquorice root pieces (mulathi) in 1 cup milk with 1/4 teaspoon saffron (kesar). Apply this paste on bald patches at bedtime continuously.

Skin and Hair Problems

- Grind fenugreek seeds (methi daana), with water and apply on the head. Leave for at least 10 minutes before washeeng. Do it every morning for a month.
- Boil 1 cup mustard oil (sarson ka tel) with 4 tablespoon henna (mehendi) leaves. Filter and bottle. (Massage on the bald patches regularly.)
- Grind the remains of tobacco smoked in a hookah and add to boiling mustard oil. Cool and store. Massage on the bald patches regularly.

Hair Greying

- Wet a lemon half and rub lemon juice into the scalp well. Wash off after it runs dry.
- Grind 1 tablespoon each, pulp of amla and lime juice. Massage this into the hair before going to bed. Wash it next morning.
- Soak shredded ginger (adrak) in honey. Eat a spoonful every morning.

Hair Thinning

- Bathe the hair in 1 cup coconut milk twice or thrice a week for a few months.

Dandruff

- Put about 21 leaves of tulsi and 10gms. of Aanwala Churna in a big bowl. Add a little of water to make a paste of them. Apply it evenly on your head and allow it to dry. Then wash it with cold water. This will prevent hair loss and clear dandruff also.
- Mix equal quantities of dried curry leaves (curry patta) lime peel (nimbu ka chilka). Shikakai, fenugreek seeds (methi daana & green gram moong saboot) and grind them finely. Store and use as a substitute for soap or shampoo.

- Apply fenugreek (methi) seeds, grind with some water and paste it on the head. Allow to soak at least for 40 minutes before washeeng. Use every morning for a month.
- Soak 2 tablespoon fenugreek seeds (methi daana) in water overnight. In the morning grind into a fine paste. Apply all over scalp and leave for 1/2 an hour. Wash with shikakai or mild shampoo.
- Boil a handful of neem leaves in 4 teacups of water. After cooling and filtering use for rinsing hair.

LICE

- Grind the seeds of neem into a fine powder and mix in some groundnut oil. Apply to the scalp. Allow it to remain overnight. Wash off next morning.
- Mix 1 teaspoon lime juice with 1 teaspoon garlic (lahsan) paste and apply on the head.
- Grind 7 to 8 almond (badam) kernels with 1 to 2 teaspoons lime juice and apply on the hair.

• • •

14

Disorders of Kidney & Urinary System

If our secretions are not proper, we can suffer from diseases like renal stone, renal failure, painful urination etc.

Painful Urination

- Carrot juice is a diuretic substance. If you have any problem connected with urination, have a glass of carrot juice every morning and evening. This will make the sufferer urinate frequently and all the problems connected with urine shall vanish. Even otherwise, drinking carrot juice would help keep the urinary tract clean and unobstructed.
- Mix 1/2 teaspoon powdered fenugreek seeds (methi daana) in buttermilk and drink.
- Add 1 tablespoon mint (pudina) leaves to 1 cup water. Take twice or thrice a day.
- Take 5 drops of sandalwood oil along with 1 cup of milk. Add a pinch of powdered carom seeds (ajwain), drink it.

Burning (Sensation During Urination)

- Powder equal quantities of liquorice (mulathi) and cumin (jeera). Take 1/4 teaspoon everyday along with 1 teaspoon honey for a month.

- Grind 2 to 3 teaspoons dried pomegranate seeds (annar daana) and take once or twice along with milk.
- Add 1 to 2 drops of sandalwood oil to milk and take as a night cap at bedtime

URINATION SCANTY

- Boil 1/4 teaspoon powdered green cardamom (chhoti illaichi) seeds in thin tea water and drink.

URINE RETENTION

- Soak a little saffron (kesar) overnight in one cup of water. Next morning drink it with 1 teaspoon honey.

BLADDER STONES

- Boil 2 figs (anjeer) in 1 cup of water. Drink daily for a month.
- For any sort of this trouble, soak about 5 to 7 gms. of tulsi seeds in water, add a little of sugar to the combination to make it more tasty. Drink this combination early in the morning and also in the afternoon, i.e. twice a day. Soon you will have copious discharge of urine and all problems connected with the urinary tract shall vanish in a week's time. Continue drinking raw milk and water mixture at least twice a day also.

KIDNEY MALFUNCTIONING

- Frequent intake of coriander (dhania) tea: boil or steep 2 teaspoons coriander (dhania) powder in a glass of boiling hot water. Add sugar and milk to taste.
- Add more almonds to the daily diet.

STONES IN THE GALL BLADDER

- Hot fomentation on the back as well as lower abdomen is always useful for relieving pain.

- To treat this problem first boil the pieces of beetroot in water and crush the pieces in this water fully. When cool, strain the potion and drink this water every morning, afternoon and evening. In about a week's time the stones will melt and pass out with urine.

BED WETTING IN CHILDREN

- Give 2 walnut halves (akhrot giri) and 1 teaspoon of kishmish to the child before sleeping for 10-12 days.

15

Disorders of Females

The female's body is a compered creation, where there are chances of many disorders. But problems like abortion are self created.

Ovary Problem

Those ladies who have this problem must eat vegetable of beetroot during their meals. If this problem is caused by some vitamin and mineral deficiency, such a diet will cure the problem very soon. All the physicians are unanimous in their choice in prescribing beetroot for such ladies.

Reproductive Weakness

- Boil 1 cup milk with 1/2 teaspoon pepper powder and to 8 crushed almonds. Take at bedtime.

Lack of Milk in Mother's Breast

- If the mother takes regular beetroot diet even before delivery she is not likely to have this problem. However if she has not done so, she must start drinking beetroot juice as the first theeng in the morning and must eat a lot of fresh beetroot as salad. In less than a week this problem will end.

Sexual Underdevelopment in Women

- 6 to 8 almonds, crushed and mixed in 1 cup milk along with 1 egg yolk, 1/2 teaspoon grind sesame seeds (til) and 1 teaspoon honey. Take once or twice a day.

Sexual Weakness

- Onion seeds (kalaunji) powdered, 1 teaspoon eaten 3 times daily along with sugar or honey.

Easy Delivery of Baby

- Mix 3 teaspoon lime juice, 1/4 teaspoon powdered black pepper and 1 teaspoon honey in 1 cup water. Drink for 3 months.

Family Planning

Device: The treatment mentioned below is especially meant for the ladies. If the lady during her menses, takes five gms. of grind turmeric and wash it down with water. She would not conceive at all. This treatment is very effective for family planning, when the couple decides not to have an issue, the wife must resort to this treatment. Or you can have copper T's or contraceptive pills. These are the safest methods without any adverse side effects.

Menstrual Disturbance

In cases of scanty discharge of menstrual blood, the main cause should be diagnosed and removed. If it is due to anaemia, the treatment of anaemia is a prerequisite to the treatment of this problem. If it is because of anaemia the treatment given above for anaemia should be adopted to.

- To cure this trouble mix beetroot in water and then squeeze the pieces to convert the whole solution to a homogenous form. Strain it through a strainer and drink it thrice or four times a day for speedy cure.

MENSTRUAL PAINS

- Boil 1 teaspoon saffron in 1/2 cup water. Let it reduce to become 1 tablespoon. Divide this decoction into three portions and take with equal quantities of water, thrice daily for a couple of days.

MENSTRUATION DELAY

- Take 1/2 teaspoon finely grind cinnamon (dalchini) every night along with 1 cup milk.
- Powder 1 teaspoon dried mint (pudina) leaves and take with 1 teaspoon honey, thrice daily.
- 6 to 8 almonds, crushed and mixed in 1 cup milk with 1 egg yolk, 1/2 teaspoon sesame (til) powder and 1 teaspoon honey. Take once or twice a day.

EXCESSIVE BLEEDING IN MENSTRUATION

- Grind the fuller's earth and mix it in 250 gms. of water. Soak it overnight. Then drink the sedimented water every morning.
- Take the rind of the Ashok Tree, about 10 gms; boil it in one kg. of milk and 250 gms of water till the quantity is halved. Then cool it and add some mishri to it to sweeten it. Have it in the morning and evening. In about a week's time the disorder shall be set right.
- Grind some bel leaves into a fine paste. Take 1 teaspoon with warm water and drink some cold water as well.
- Grind 10 fresh buds of figs(anjeer) and apply on the lower abdomen below the navel for a few hours. Repeat this frequently.

- Boil 1 tablespoon coriander (dhania) seeds in 2 cups of water till it is reduced to 1 cup. Add sugar to taste and drink when lukewarm. Repeat twice or thrice a day.

STOPPAGE OF MENSTRUATION

- Take about 10 gms. of carrot seed and 20gms of jaggery and boil in 500 gms of water till the water is reduced to one third of its normal quantity. Then strain the water and ask the afflicted lady to drink it twice daily, about 2 spoonfuls. In a couple of days the bleeding would commence in the normal cycle.

Take 10 gms of black til, gokhru 10 gms. and mix both in about 250 gms. of water. Drink the water twice daily, about 2 teaspoonfuls every time.

MORNING SICKNESS

- Mix juice of 15-20 tender curry leaves (curry patta) with 2 teaspoon lime juice and 1 teaspoon sugar. Take in the morning.
- Mix 1/8 teaspoon nutmeg (jaiphal) powder with 1 tablespoon freshly extracted amla juice. Take 3 times a day.
- 1/2 teaspoon ginger (adrak) juice with 1 teaspoon each fresh mint (pudina) juice mixed with a tablespoon of honey, take frequently.
- Mix 1 teaspoon each fresh juice of mint (pudina) and lime along with 1 tablespoon honey. Take 3 times a day.

LACTATION IN MOTHERS

- Mix together 1 teaspoon each cumin (jeera) powder & sugar and take with warm milk after dinner every day for a few days.

- Boil 2 teaspoon cumin (jeera) seed in 1/2 cup water. Filter it. Mix in 1/2 cup milk and 1 teaspoon honey. Drink once a day for a few days.
- Boil 2 teaspoon fennel seeds (saunf) in barley water and take twice or thrice a day.
- Frequently, cook unripe papayas (kachcha Papita) and eat.
- 1/2 teaspoon finely grind cinnamon (dalchini) taken at night along with 1 cup milk.

Leucorrhoea

It is a symptom of many diseases peculiar to women, It consists of white watery discharge from private part of the lady.

- Take shivallingi (a root) and grind and sieve it. Have 5 gms. of this powder everyday with milk as the first theeng in the morning for the desired result.
- Grind 10 gms. of turmeric and boil it in 100 gms. of water. When cold, wash the private part at least thrice a day with this water. Besides this take a batasha, put about 8 to 10 drops of the milk of a Banyan and swallow it daily before sunrise for about a week. During this time the ladies should avoid physical contact with their husbands. Even otherwise they should observe continence and lead an ascetic's life till they are fully cured. Any physical contact, in such condition might infect their husband's body too.
- The dried and powdered bark of the Mulsari (mimusops Elengi) tree mixed with an equal weight of raw sugar should be taken in nine grams dose every morning with water. Alternatively, equal weights of the leaf shoots of Bastard Teak (Dhak) and Banyan tree should be dried and powdered. An equal quantity of raw sugar should be mixed with them and nine gram doses should be taken with 250 ml. milk thrice daily. The root of the silk cotton tree is

another specific herb for this condition. Seven grams of its powder with an equal weight of raw sugar should be taken with a glass of milk. Or, dry amla and liquorice in equal quantities and powdered and mixed with thrice the quantity of honey make an effective drug against the disease.

Regimen: A strict dietary regimen is needed: fried foods and spices, pickles and savouries should be avoided. The patient should take betelnut after meals as it has curative effect. Late night and sexual inter course are of course taboo during the course of disease.

Amenorrhoea

- A week before the period of a women are due, a decoction of six grams of flex seeds, about 250ml. of water reduced to half through boiling mixed with 20 grams of jaggery and 20 grams of ghee should be taken daily. Alternatively a decoction of ten grams of seeds of carrot and jaggery should be taken for about a week. Another remedy is to boil six grams of baberang (Embelia Ribes) three grams of dry ginger and 20 grams of jaggery in 500 ml. of water till half of it is left. The decoction should be taken for some days. It shows its effect.
- Decoction of 20grams each of flowers and leaves of the cotton plant (500ml. of water boiled to half its quantity) mixed with 20 grams of jaggery is also effective in inducing the menstrual flow. Another remedy is to steep 10 grams of black sesame seeds and an equal quantity of small galtrops (Gokhru) in 250 ml. of water and to grind them in the same water. It should be sweetened with sugar and drunk.

Dysmenorrhoea

- One hundred grams of juice of green leaves of black Nightshade (mako) and leaves of Chicory (Kasni) should be placed on fire and when it coagulates, it should be strained and drunk after mixing 20 grams of Jaggery with it. Twenty grams of the leaves of the following eight herbs are boiled in water (i) Sambhalu (Indian wild pepper), (ii) Saheengana (horse radish), (iii) Bakayan (Indian Lilac) (iv) Kasni (wild Chicory) (v) Mako (Black Nightshade) (vi) Khatmi (Marsh Mallow), (vii) Narma Kapas (cotton plant) and (viii) Soya (dill). When the leaves are cooked and the water evaporated, they should be fried in sesame oil like any vegetable and tied to the lower abdomen like a poultice. It will deal effectively with inflammation.

- A very helpful remedy for the pain of dysmenorrhoea is a decoction of root of Cotton Tree (18grams), Telia Geru (6grams) leaves of Rose Bush (6grams), Root of Chaulai (6grams), Gur (24grams) boiled in 750 ml. of water till one eighth is left. The decoction should be taken for three days continuously. Alternatively, 120milligrams of the drug may be kept in the vagina to find relief.

Menorrhagia and Metrorrhagia

If there is excessive discharge of blood from the womb during the monthly periods, it is called menorrhagia, but if there is irregularity of menstruation, the condition is called metrorrhagia. The treatment for both the conditions is the same.

- The disorders may be due to the imbalance of the hormones, abnormal growths (whether benign or malignant) in the uterus may be at the root of excessive or irregular bleeding. In severe cases, bleeding may continue for a long time giving rise to symptoms of prostration like giddiness, constant headaches, pain in the calves and restlessness. Neglect of the condition or ineffective attempts at dealing with it may lead to anaemia of the most severe type. Saraca Indica and Lodhra (symplocos racemasa) are two remedies which have been successfully used by the practitioners of Ayurveda to deal with these conditions. A home remedy is to grind seven leaves of the pomegranate tree and seven grains of rice into a paste and given to the patient for a month twice daily. It acts as a curative as well as a preventive agent.

- Twenty grams of bark of Ashoka tree should be crushed and boiled in 250 ml. of milk and equal amount of water. When half of the liquid is left, it should be strained, sweetened with sugar and drunk. A few days use will put the patient on the road to recovery. Or, equal weight of Pathani Lodh Red Ochre (geru) and Oak Galls (Mazu) should be finely powdered and four grams of it taken in the morning and evening with milk.
- Half ripe fruits of the country fig tree (Gular) should be dried in the shade, powdered and mixed with an equal quantity of sugar. Six grams of the powder taken with milk in the morning and evening gives relief. Alternatively, three grams of Rasaut and an equal quantity of shellac should be finely grind together and made into two doses, one to be taken with milk in the morning and evening.

Another wonderful remedy for this condition is Amla. Dry Amla should be soaked in juice of green Amla for three days and then grind into powder. Six grams of this powder taken with cow's milk for some days cures the conditions.

Other remedies recommended are 10 grams each of selkhari (chalk) and geru (red ochre) grind together should be taken in three grams doses thrice daily.

Multani Mitti steeped in water and the supernatant water drunk in the morning is also good for excessive bleeding from the womb. Five grams of bark of kurchi and raw sugar mixed together taken in the morning and evening is also an effective remedy.

ABORTION

Take about three to four medium sized radishes and boil them in water. Add 100 gms. water for each radish and boil it by steam. When water becomes dry, squeeze the radish and add soft leaves of radish to it also. Do not add salt. Instead add a little of sugarcandy. The lady should have it twice a day.

•••

16

Disorders of Male and Aphrodisiacs (Bajikaran)

Male disorders include impotence, early ejaculation and sexually transmitted diseases (Std's) besides physical weakness.

TESTES PROBLEM

- It there be swelling on the testes or any other problem concerning with testes, apply the paste prepared in the following manner over the testes. Take about 5 gms. each of a camel's dung. Amarbel (easily available in Mango groves), the leaves of Arhar and tulsi leaves, grind them to a homogeneous paste in a little of cow's urine, when the paste is ready, apply it over the testes thickly. Allow it to dry and remove it in the morning. A week's treatment will cure all troubles connected with the testes.

VENEREAL DISEASE (GONORRHOEA)

- Juice of tulsi leaves is very effective to cure all sort of these troubles. Take 5 gms. each of tulsi seeds or dried tulsi leaves, Kalami shora and the grains of small cardamom. Grind them together to powder form. Have this combination (just 1/2 a gm.) with 100 gms. Kacchi Lassi (raw milk and water combination). Add water twice the amount of milk. Drink this lassi with that powder thrice or four times a day. But don't add either salt or sugar in the lassi. About a fortnight long this treatment shall get you cured from any sort of veneral disease.

Nocturnal Ejaculation

- Grind the dry ginger and add sugar to it. Have this powder everyday in the morning. First eat the powder (about 10 gms.) daily and wash it down with 100 gms. of milk.
- Take about 5 gms. of mishri with 100 gms of milk in the night or morning.
- Take a glass of cold water as the first theeng in the morning after you have cleared your bowels.
- Take mochras, kamarkas, khus-khus (kinds of poppy seeds) and 6 gms. of Bishop's seeds. Grind and sieve them to a powdered form. Take this powder daily with 250 gms. of milk for quick relief.
- A glass of cold water on an empty stomach in the morning is highly recommended. Ten grams of dry corriander grind in water and sweetened with sugar should be taken in the morning.
- Six grams of leafshoots of acacia grinded in water also help this condition.
- A sufferer from nocturnal pollutions must take exercise in the evening (before dinner) so that he becomes too tired to dream and has a sound sleep.

Deteriorating Sexual Potency

- Take 30gms. washed Urad Dal and fry it in pure ghee. Then mix it in 300 gms. of milk and thicken it to kheer form. Then add sugar as required and eat it hot. This kheer is very efficacious to enhance your sexual potency.
- Take white Mossali 25 gms. Isabgol Bhusi 40 gms. and grind and sieve both to get a soft powder. Cook the whole

Disorders of Male and Aphrodisiacs (Bajikaran) 133

lot in about 300 gms. of milk. Add sugar and have it daily in the night after your dinner to enhance your sexual potency.
- Take 2 teaspoons of amla juice and mix it with two teaspoonfuls each honey and lime juice. Add 1 teacup water and drink on an empty stomach every morning. (Attention: The treatment should continue for at least 120 days to achieve expected results.)

Boil 1 teaspoon grind fenugreek seeds (methi dana) in a cup of water and drink.
- 1/2 teaspoon ginger (adrak) juice mixed with honey and a semi boiled egg, taken at night.

Mix 1/4 teaspoon nutmeg (jaiphal) powder in a teaspoon honey and take milk an hour before going to bed.
- Onion seeds (kalaunji) dried and powdered, 1 teaspoon eaten 3 times daily along with sugar or honey.
- Take about 100 gms. of the seeds of radish. Dry them fully then pound them to powder form. Now strain them through a fine but coarse cloth. Start taking 5 gms. of this powder with 100gms. of butter. If butter is not available, you can have it with cream as well, in about 10 days' time you shall be again virile. But continue the treatment for atleast one month.

Fry equal quantities of carom (ajwain) seeds and kernel of tamarind seeds (imli ke beej) in ghee. Powder this mixture and store in a dry, cool place. Mix 1 teaspoon of this powder in a glass of milk along with 1 tablespoon honey. Drink daily at bedtime.
- Soak 8 to 10 almonds and 1 teaspoon rice overnight. Remove the outer skin. Grind into a fine paste. Mix in some milk and a pinch of turmeric (haldi) powder. Boil and drink along with sugar candy (mishri) or ordinary sugar to taste.

- Mix ¼ teaspoon saffron (kesar) with milk. Take twice daily.

Premature Ejaculation

- Take 10 gms. pure ghee 5 gms. honey, grind liquorice 10 gms. Make a paste of all the three and lick it regularly. Wash it down with 250 gms. of milk. Have it after the intercourse.
- Grind dry coriander seeds. Mix it with 'missri' and have about 5 gms. of this powder washed down with cold water.
- Take basil seeds 50 gms; sugar 50gms. and grind and sieve the whole lot. Take just 6 gms. of this powder, and drink it with 100 gms. of milk early in the morning.
- Take the seeds of Lajwanti plant and mix it with equal amount of sugar. Take 5 gms. of this mixture and wash it down with 100 gms. of milk. This combination thickens the semen and stops early ejaculation. Write your problem at drs108@gmail.com

Impotence

Impotence is a disorder peculiar to males: in females the corresponding disorder is known as frigidity (the absence of sexual desire and a failure to respond to sexual stimulii). Impotence may be defined as the inability to perform the sex act or incomplete performance (premature ejaculation) which leaves the female partner dissatisfied. Impotence may be organic or functional. Among the organic causes are lesions of the external genitals, i.e. a tight foreskin, disturbance of the endocrine glands, such as diminished activity of the gonads (as happens in old age.) diseases of the nervous system, diabetes, alcoholism.Among the psychological factors are ignorance, fear, weakness of sexual desire or a guilt complex which may inhibit the action of the gonads.

It has been found that in a majority of the males suffering from impotence, the reasons are psychological. They may be suffering from a guilt complex because they may have indulged in masturbation, unnatural sex or incest (sexual relations with near kindered) during their early life. Or, they might be always thinking of sex, being in an agitated state of mind all the time and suffer from premature ejaculation. If the reasons for impotence are psychological only a proper psychoanalysis of the patient will help. It could be explained to the sufferer that having masturbated in early life does not sexually incapacitate a male. But after all the psychological methods have been tried, the following remedies should be used:

- In case of spermatorrhoes (ejaculation even without the penis having attained tumescence), tender, seedless pods of Acacia should be dried in the shade and powdered before being mixed with an equal weight of raw sugar. Six grams of it should be taken with milk in the morning.
- Leaf shoots of Banyan tree may be substituted for acacia pods.
- Cotton tree dried in the shade and powdered before mixing it with an equal amount of raw sugar should be taken in 10 grams dose with milk.
- Fifty grams each of Kernels of seeds of Bastard Teak (Dhak) and siris tree finely grind and mixed with 50 gms. of raw sugar should be taken in six grams dose every morning for three weeks to relieve the condition. Fifty grams each of dry amla and mango, ginger, Amba Haldi should be powdered and mixed with an equal weight of raw sugar. The daily morning dose is six grams, taken with milk write your problem at drs108 @ gmail. com.

Physical Weakness

- Soak 2 or 3 dried figs (anjeer) overnight in 1 cup water. Eat them along with 1 tablespoon honey the next morning. Continue for a month.
- Fry in 1 tablespoon butter, 2 teaspoons each wheat flour, almond paste and poppy seeds (khuskhus) paste. Eat this along with 1 cup boiled leaves of fenugreek (methi).

•••

17

High Blood Pressure & Other Heart Problems

Now a days as our life is becoming fast, we are over stressed and suffer from disorders like hypertension. The patient should stop taking or reduce as much as taking salt. He should have easily digestible food minus spicy condiments.

- She/He should have as much water as possible. Sometimes it is due to the malfunctioning of kidneys. Lot of water intake will help curing the basic defect.
- She/He should avoid taking tea, cigarettes, coffee and rich creamy biscuits.
- She/He should try to do light exercise and resort to massage of the body if possible.
- Have as much fruits as possible instead of regular food.
- The patient should try to keep his bowels clean. Constipation adds to the impurities in the body and thus put extra load on the expulsion system of the body.

Giddiness due to Blood Pressure

- Soak 1 teaspoon each of powdered amla, coriander seeds (saboot dhania) and sandalwood in a cup of water overnight. Strain and drink the next day. Continue for a few days.

HYPERTENSION

- Drink curry leaves (curry patta) juice initially 3 times a day (1 glassful) for 1-2 months and then reduce to only once in the morning. Have it on empty stomach. For taking out juice, fill your mixer with washed curry leaves, add 1/2 - 3/4 glass water. Churn well and sieve. Add 1/2-1 lemon juice and drink fresh.
- A few cloves of garlic if taken on an empty stomach not only corrects the condition known as flatulence, but also lowers high blood pressure.
- The best remedy for hypertension is, sarpagandha (Rauwolfia Serpentina, which has been used in India for many years to deal with nervous disorders like insanity and high blood pressure. Alkaloids of this drug which have a direct effect on hypertension have been isolated and are being widely used by the practitioners of modern medicine, but they have certain unpleasant side effects which the drug taken in raw form does not have. Practitioners of Indian systems of medicine have therefore, preferred to use the root of the drug in a powdered form. Half a teaspoonful of this drug taken thrice a day deals with hypertension effectively.
- Drink coriander (dhania) juice made from fresh dhania (same way as curry leaves juices) 3 times a day. If this is not effective, start, having fenugreek (methi) juice instead (made from fresh methi) and if this is also not effective, move to curry leaves juice. Drink each juice for 10-12 days at least before you decide. If it is not working then move to the next one.

LOW BLOOD PRESSURE

- Have juice of basil (tulsi) leaves (10-15) mixed 1 teaspoon honey.

- Add 3/4 cup crushed liquorice (Mulathi) root to 4 cups cold water and allow it to stand for 2 hours. Then bring it quickly to a boil and steep for 5 minutes. Add this to the bathwater in the tub.
- Brandy or Alcohol of any variety in quantity from 15 to 50 ml diluted with warm water, is a temporary expedient which can be tried till the exact cause of the malady is ascertained. Or, spirit of Ammonia Aroma should be given in teaspoonful doses diluted with an equal amount of water.

HIGH CHOLESTEROL

- Sunflower seeds contain a substantial amount of linoelic acid which is helpful in reducing cholesterol deposits on the walls of the arteries.
- Finely dice an onion and mix it with 1 cup buttermilk along with 1/4 teaspoon black pepper (kali mirch) powder and drink.
- Regularly intake garlic (lahsan) cloves for a few days.
- Regularly intake coriander (dhania) decoction made by boiling 2 teaspoons dry coriander seeds (dhania) powder in 1 cup water. (milk and sugar can be added to impove its taste. This could be a welcome substitute for teas or coffee.)

COLOURLESS NAILS

Nails are the mirror of one's health. Their getting disfigured or colourless or brittle is a sure indication of sometheeng being wrong in the system. Normally the lack of calcium and vitamin D in body is usually manifest through the nails. Since beetroot supplies these nutrients, such persons must consume beetroot as much as they can both as salad and as vegetable. In winters if after eating beetroots one cares to sit in the sun, Vitamin D's deficiency shall be made good soon.

INSOMNIA

- Give to patient just one leaf of tulsi for chewing it and spread rest of the leaves evenly below his pillow and the corners of bed below the bedsheet. As the smell of tulsi leaves strikes his nostril, the person will feel sleepy and soon he will fall into sleep.
- Fry cumin seeds in a little ghee & grind to a powder. A teaspoon of fried powder of cumin seeds (jeera) mixed with the pulp of a ripe banana should be taken at night regularly.
- 2 teaspoons juice of fenugreek (methi) leaves alongwith 1 teaspoon honey may be taken daily.

Soak 1 tablespoon leaves of fresh mint(pudina) in 1 cup water for 30 minutes. Drink it every night. (do not boil).

- Take seeds of watermelon and white poppy seeds (khuskhus) and grind them separately. Mix equal amount by weight. Have 3/4 teaspoon once in the morning and once before sleeping. Take for 1-3 weeks as needed.
- Have raw onion with meals particularly with dinner.
- Consume plenty of curd. Also massage head with curd before washeeng. This is very helpful.
- Add 2 teaspoons of honey to a big cupful of water and have it before going to bed. Babies generally fall asleep after having honey.
- A cup of warm milk sweetened with honey should be taken before going to bed. Have it everyday.
- Juice of celery leaves (ajwain ka patta) with thick ribs & brittle stalks mixed with a tablespoon of honey when had at night before retiring helps to relax into a restful sleep.

Angina Pectoris

- Thoroughly mix 2 teaspoons almond oil with 1 teaspoon rose oil. Rub gently on the chest, morning and evening
- Boil 1 teaspoon fenugreek seeds (methi daana) in 1/2 cup water. Strain and add 2 teaspoons honey. Take twice daily.

Heart Attack

- Take 1/2 teaspoon garlic (lahsan) powder everyday.

Heart Burn

- Add 1 tablespoon mint (pudina) leaves to 1 cup water. Take twice or thrice a day.

Heart Pain

- Boil 1/2 teaspoon sandalwood powder in 1 cup water. Drink thrice daily.

Heart Palpitation

- Boil 1/4 teaspoon powdered cardamom (chhoti illaichi) seeds in tea water and drink.

Heart Weakness

- Regular intake of ripe bananas strengthens the heart.

Heart Troubles

- Tulsi is very effective to cure all sort of heart troubles. Since it controls blood pressure and keeps blood clean, its regular consumption prevents heart attacks. For special tonic for heart, prepare the medicine in the following way. Take about 1 gm. dried powder of tulsi leaves, add 3 gms of the powder of Arjun tree and mix even amount of honey. Now either churn or mix them till the solution is fully homogeneous. Take about 1 gm. of this paste, add a little

more of honey and lick it at least thrice a day, preferable early in the morning as the first theeng an hour after lunch and as the last theeng before your retiring for the day.
- Eat 1/4 teaspoon asafoetida (heeng) along with one large raisin (munakka) everyday.

Tachycardia (Palpitation)
- Concoction of sevati (rosa alba) flowers, preserve of apple or carrots, in a dose of ten grams in silver foil should be eaten daily for some days. Or, carrots may be buried in hot ashes: when tender they should be taken out sliced and placed in open overnight in a ceramic dish to catch the dew. In the morning they should be sprinkled with sugar and rose water and eaten for some days regularly. Equal weights of aniseed, dry coriander and jaggery (gur) should be powdered and taken in six grams doses after each meal. Five grams of aniseed. Three of coriander and 11 pieces of raisins should be steeped in water or rose water overnight and strained in the morning before drinking.

Anaemia

Anaemia or the lack of red blood corpuscles and haemoglobins is called Pandurog in Ayurveda. It may be caused by loss of blood through excessive menstruation, injury or any other cause in which excessive bleeding takes place, or due to defective blood formation because of injections, toxins and drugs or the inadequate intake of iron.
- Since beetroot is rich in iron it helps in enhancing the quantity of blood in the system. If one takes adequate amount of chukandar (beetroot) in salad or as vegetable this trouble gets cured in about a month. Having lemon juice drenched beetroot pieces as the first thing in morning is an ideal way of checking out the blood in body. Especially

the ladies must consume beetroot in this manner during their periods.
- Soak 10-12 currants (munakkas) in water overnight. Remove seeds and eat them. Have for 2-4 weeks.
- Have spinach juice of 125 gm. spinach everyday, for 2-3 weeks.
- Foods rich in iron- honey, almonds, bananas, apricot (khumani), raisins (kishmish), fenugreek or salad leaves, onion, spinach (paalak), grapes, tomatoes, carrots, gooseberry (amla), beetroots (chukander), apples, pomegranate (anaar). Have plenty of them if you are anaemic.
- Carrot is a very rich source of iron and if taken raw with a few pieces of chukander (beetroot) it is certain to remove this trouble. Have fresh carrots and beetroot, liberally sprinkled over with lemon juice and munch your way to pink state of health. Vitamin 'A' and 'C' would not only keep your body strong but your blood red without any impurity. This is the surest cure of anaemia.
- Mix 1 tablespoon amla juice mashed with a ripe banana and eat 2-3 times a day.
- Have a ripe banana with 1 tablespoon honey, 1-2 times a day.
- Take freshly prepared apple juice an hour before meals or just before retiring for the night. For proper absorption of the juice, remember the stomach should be relatively empty when you have juice and also do not take anytheeng for about half an hour after the juice.
- Avoid drinking tea and coffee immediately after meals as the tannin present in these interferes in the absorption of iron from food.

Blood Deficiency

- Take 2 teaspoons of amla juice and mix it with two teaspoonfuls each of honey and lime. Add 1 teacup water and drink on an empty stomach every morning. Whenever fresh fruits are not available, dried amla can be used. Soak 1 tablespoon the previous night in a cup of water. (Note: The treatment should continue for at least 120 days to achieve expected results.)
- Mix 1 tablespoon juice of amla with a ripe mashed banana and eat twice or thrice a day.
- Soak 2 or 3 dried figs (anjeer) in 1 tea cup water. Eat them along with milk next morning for a month.

Giddiness

- Soak cumin seeds (jeera) in lime juice overnight. Keep this mixture under the sun till completely dry. Bottle it. Chew 1/2 teaspoon of this mixture and drink with a glass of warm water.

• • •

Different Fevers

Fever is a general term. There are several types of fever like malaria, typhoid, viral etc.

Malaria

Malaria is a fever common to tropical and sub tropical regions, particularly, places which are moist and dirty. The causative parasite enters the blood stream through the bite of a particular variety of mosquito. It has three distinct symptoms: feeling of chilliness, onset of fever and profuse sweating when the fever subsides. The treatments are the following:

- First administer light purgative to purge the system of the filth. The patient should have as much water as possible.
- Take basil leaves 10 gms and 7 grains of black pepper. Grind them to powder form. Sieve it through a thick cloth. Mix it in about 100 gms. of water and ask the patient have this water at least twice daily, preferably on empty stomach.
- Edible lime 5 gms, mixed in about 50 gms of water. Then add the juice of one fresh lime. Administer this sedimented water to the patient at least thrice daily for quick relief. Administer this water especially when the fever is showing its presence in the body.

- Roast alum and then grind it to the powdered form. Mix it with grinded khand and administer daily with four hourly interval.

TYPHOID

In this fever there is an insidious fever, a typical course of temperature, marked by abdominal symptoms consisting of ulceration of the bowels, an eruption of the skin for uncertain duration and a liability to frequent relapses. The following treatment is very effective to cure it.

- The patient should be well looked after. No solid food should be given to the patient. Only easily digestible fruits like sweet lime, oranges, etc. may be given. He must be placed in a clean and airy room.
- Take two grains of Unnab, Munnakka 4, Kuhbkalan 3 gms. and Misri 10 gms. grind all of them and mix in 100 gms of pure water, preferably boiled and cooled. Strain the water and make the patient drink at four hourly interval.
- Take 4 basil leaves, saffron 7 shreds, 7 grains of black pepper. Grind them to a paste by adding water and form small tablets out of the whole lot. Take each tablet twice or thrice everyday with lukewarm milk. The fever would also subside and the patient would get the desired relief.
- 1 to 2 teaspoons fresh juice of coriander leaves (hara dhania) is mixed in 1 cup buttermilk and taken 2-3 times.
- Mash a ripe banana along with 1 tablespoon honey and eat twice a day for a few days.

FLU

- Take about 10 gms of tulsi leaves and 250 gms of water. Boil them together till water is halved. Now add in the remaining water rock salt, according to taste. No sooner did you start to sweat that the effect of flu shall be removed with the sweat and you shall be alright. Alternatively drink karha of tulsi leaves, black pepper in batasha for still quicker relief.

INFLUENZA

Influenza is an acute disease similar to all fevers. Its cardinal symptoms are: high temperature, aches over whole of the body, stiffness of the limbs and a sore throat.

(i) Keep the patient in a clean and airy place. Have the room incensed to drive out the germs from the atmosphere.

(ii) Make the patient eat only easily digestible food like moong dal, or sago kheer. Don't let him take anytheeng cold. Avoid all those things that generate phlegm in the body.

- Ask the patient to smell a piece of camphor after every hour.
- Make him do gargles with hot saline water.
- Take basil leaves 10 gms., cloves 6 gms, salt as per the taste and boil the whole lot in about 250 gms. of water. When the quantity of water is halved due to boiling, strain it and ask the patient to drink it at four hourly interval.
- Take Bishop's seeds (ajwain) and cinnamon in equal measure and boil both of them in about 500 gms. of water. When the water remains half of its original quantity, strain and give it to patient to drink at four hourly interval.

PNEUMONIA

Pneumonia is the inflammation of the substance of lungs which manifests itself in many forms. The attack usually commences with shivering (in young children with convulsions), followed by pain in the chest and sometimes vomiting. The temperature rises suddenly to 104°F and the pulse is extremely rapid. The breatheeng is shallow and rapid. If there is expectoration of phlegm, it is rusty. There is profuse sweating at the time and the pain may abate as the disease progresses. Try the following remedy:

- Take the root of the Arand (the plant from which castor oil is made) about 10 gms; dry ginger 3 gms and boil both in water till the quantity of the water remains 3/4 of the original quantity. Now strain the water and ask the patient to drink it, followed by 20 gms. of pure honey.
- Massage with turpentine oil brings great relief to the patient. But don't do the massage in an open space. It will remove the pain and congestion in the ribs.
- Take the root of kareer plant, grind it and boil in water for half an hour. Then sponge the whole body of the patient with this water. Cover his body with a blanket immediately after the sponge.

FEVERISHNESS

- Mix 1 teacup fresh lemon juice in tender coconut water and drink.

FEVER OF EVERY TYPE

- Boil 2 tablespoons fennel seeds (saunf) in 1 teacup water till it is reduced to half. Filter it. Take 1 tablespoon every morning and evening for a few days. (This filtrate, when used to wash the eyes frequently, is reported to strengthen the eye muscles. It is a good cleaning lotion for inflamed eyes.)
- Grind a few root of the mango tree into a fine paste and apply on the palm and soles of the patient.

- The neem leaf decoction taken with pepper powder lowers temperature.
- ½ teaspoon grind pepper mixed in warm water along with 1 teaspoon palm candy (sugar obtained from palm). This drink is taken at bedtime.
- Extract 1 teaspoon each juice of tulsi leaves and bel flowers. Add 1 teaspoon honey. Take twice a day.
- Tea made by boiling 1 teaspoon fenugreek seeds (methi daana). Taken twice or thrice a day provides excellent remedy. (A little honey or lemon juice can be added to improve the flavour).

Fever of Unknown Origin

- Boil 1 tablespoon tulsi leaves with 1 teaspoon powdered cardamom (chhoti illaichi) in 2 teacups water. Take 1 cup of this decoction with milk and sugar to taste, 2 or 3 times a day.

Note : The above mentioned medicines for different disorders can be used at a primary health care level and also as preventives. Most of these conditions need very systematic treatment. So please get the advice of a good physician for specific, severe and prolonged illness.

• • •

Part – III

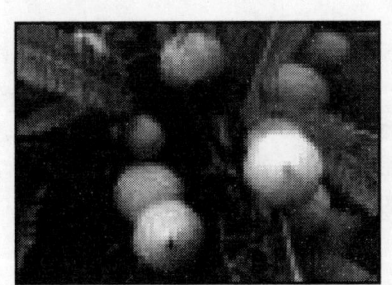

19

Different Tastes

There are six tastes: sweet, sour, salty, pungent, bitter and astringent and each is derived from two of the five elements. The tastes are important in seeing how "we are what we eat." Our bodies are formed by the elemental nature of our intake which increases or decreases doshic (VPK) balance

Sweet is made from the elements earth and water; it increases Kapha (also made from earth and water), and decreases Pitta and Vata. Sweet is found in sugars, carbohydrates, fats, oils and amino acids. Its characteristics are heavy, cold and oily. While it builds tissue, it also can block ducts and channels, and its cold nature dampens the digestive fire. Over indulgence in the "sweetness of life" produces Kapha illnesses such as obesity, diabetes, blocked circulation indigestion, and respiratory congestion. On the emotional level, sweet provides satisfaction unless over consumed, where it causes complacency and laziness and feeds greed and dissatisfaction (when sweets ferment they turn sour).

Sour is created from the elements earth and fire. It increases Pitta and Kapha but decreases Vata. Sour is found in acid fruits (sour), acid vegetables (ascorbic acid), alcohol (oxalic acid), fermented products, cultured dairy products (lactic acid), and to a lesser extent, proteins (amino acids) and oils (fatty acids).

Its properties are heavy, hot and oily. It strengthens digestive fire, and is contraindicated in gastritis, ulcers, inflammation, wasting and other Pitta disturbances. It stimulates appetite and digestion, increases waste elimination and reduces spasms. Sour is associated with envy, jealousy and dissatisfaction; the opposite of sweet. "Sour grapes" metaphorically refers to desire turning to distaste.

Salty is composed from the elements of water and fire. It increases Pitta and Kapha and decreases Vata. It is found in concentrated form in rock salt, sea salt and in diluted forms in sea foods and the mineral salts in vegetables and fruits. If over indulged, it causes inflammation, swelling, fluid retention, wrinkling and early aging. In proper amounts it is important in digestion, appetite, electrolyte balance and elimination. Salt increases our zest and enjoyment of life and reduces fear and anxiety. But the effect of overuse on the mind and emotions is hedonism- craving sensation, anger at obstruction to indulgence or physical pleasure (like an "old salt" on leave from his ship).

Pungent is formed from the elements fire and air, and increases Pitta and Vata while reducing Kapha. Pungent is characteristicaly heating, light, and dry and is found in spices and concentrated in essential oils (volatiles and aromatics). Pungent functions to stimulate secretions and digestive enzymes, increase appetite and metabolism. It is a treatment for Kapha disorders(obesity, stagnant circulation, diabetes, coughs, respiratory congestion) and aids in the elimination through the skin. Used in excess, it causes or increases pain, thirst, burning, impotence, faintness and debility. Mentally and emotionally, it creates extroversion and the need for stimulation and increases irritability and anger.

Bitter is created by the elements air and ether. It increases Vata (air and ether) and decreases Pitta and Kapha. It is cooling, light and dry and is found in bitter green leafy vegetables (dandelion and endive), bitter herbs (golden seal and gentian) and bitter roots (turmeric). At normal consumption, it purifies and dries secretions, tones and tightens tissue. It is helpful for decreased appetite, digestive problems, fever, liver and skin irritations. Over indulgence can cause all Vata disorders, including nerve irritations, weight loss, dryness, cracking skin, and lack of secretions. Emotionally, it produces dissatisfaction and realization of the need to change ("the bitter truth"). It reduces anger and complacency, but in excess can produce bitter obstinance, frustration, grief and insecurity.

Astringent is composed of the elements air and earth. It increases Vata and decreases Pitta and Kapha, because the air component overrides the earth influence. Astringent is found in tannins, barks, and resins (oak bark, myrrh) and astringent herbs and vegetables (beans, potatoes, alfalfa) and raw honey. In small amounts it reduces secretions, tightens and purifies body tissue. In excess it dries secretions and tissues causing constipation, thirst, tremors and tingling. Emotionally, in overuse, it causes introversion, separateness, fear and anxiety.

SUMMARY OF TASTES

Through understanding taste and its influence on our doshic nature and metabolism, we can choose foods and essential oils to understand our cravings and emotions and balance ourselves. Western diet over emphasizes sweet, sour and salty foods and produces a society which is greedy, indulgent, hedonistic and increasingly dissatisfied. A personal step toward change can be "tasting the bitter truth," looking inward and seeking balance through taste.

Therapeutic Use Of Tastes

Taste (Rasa)	Vata (Air)	Element (Dosha) Pitta (Fire)	Kapha (Water)
Sweet	destroys	destroys	increases
Sour	destroys	increases	increases
Salt	destroys	increases	increases
Bitter	increases	destroys	destroys
Hot	increases	increases	destroys
Pungent	increases	destroys	destroys

• • •

20

Role of Food in Balancing the Doshas

Lifestyle and diet play important role in balancing doshas Fortunately, essential oils can help create changes in lifestyle and can be added to the diet. This chapter is intended as a quick reference guide to assist in your day to day living.

REDUCING VATA

General Information: Consume warm foods and drinks, unctuous (oily) food, foods with predominately sweet, sour and salty tastes. Oil your body every day with sesame and essential oils. It is best not to eat alone. Best colours for meditation are yellow, orange, red. Avoid dark colours. Best stones are jade, peridot. Best metal is gold. Avoid cold wind, dampness, excess travel, television, radio, movies, excess talking and thinking. Practice yoga that is calming and grounding. Exercise should be non-vigorous and non-exhaustive, such as tai chi, walking or swimming. Use bulk and tonic laxatives like flax seed and psyllium. Avoid diet and fasting, dry foods, cold foods and drinks and foods having predominately pungent, bitter or astringent tastes. Meals should be small but frequent. It is important to go to bed before 10 p.m. If prone to insomnia, drink teas at night that are calming and sootheeng. Vata types do better in warm, moist climates. When they live in a cold climate, it is important to protect the head, neck and chest, and keep warm. Use routines to ground, calm and stabilize your life.

Reducing Pitta

General Information : Cool foods and drinks are best; foods with predominately sweet, bitter and astringent tastes. Avoid food with pungent, sour and salty tastes. Have flowers around the house. Bathe in moonlight. Take walks in the cool air. At night, massage your scalp with coconut oil. Competitive team sports, which promote cooperation are ideal; also activities like hiking which are vigorous and not ego-producing. The best stones, to be carried on the right side of the body, are sapphire, aquamarine, azurite. Take flower baths. Do regular liver flushes; juice of 1 lemon, 1 tbl. olive oil, 1 small diced apple or other fruit, blend and drink instead of breakfast (Vata and Kapha may add ginger, garlic and cayenne). Follow diet and avoid restricted foods whenever possible. For meditation colours, use blue and green. Best metal to use on the body is silver. Avoid excessive sauna, hot tub or sunbatheeng. Seek out what gives you joy.

Reducing Kapha

General Information: Fast once a week for twenty-four hours. Foods with pungent, bitter and astringent tastes are best. Avoid or reduce sweet, sour and salty foods. No breakfast before 10 a.m., light meal in the evening. Frequent physical and mental exercise; sexual intercourse, minimum sleep. Best colours are yellow, brown and red. Best stones are yellow topaz, coral and diamond. Best metals to use on the body are copper or iron. Take regular baths and saunas to promote sweating.

• • •

21

Reducing Imbalance by Diets

DIET FOR REDUCING VATA IMBALANCE

YES		AVOID/REDUCE	
(cooked well) Grains		barley	granola
basmati rice	oats	buckwheat	millet
brown rice	wheat	corn	no dry cereals

Fruits

avocado	mango	apple	melon
banana	melons	cranberry	pear
cantaloupe	papaya	dried fruits	pomegranate
cherries	peaches		
coconut	persimmons		
fresh figs	sweet berries		
grapes	sweet fruits		
grapefruit	sweet orange		
lemon	sweet		
lime	pineapple		
mandarin	sweet plums		

Vegetables

Well cooked vegetables		bean sprouts	eggplant
(with butter, lemon)		broccoli	green beans
beets	sweet potato	brussels	lettuce

159

carrots	tomatoes	sprouts	peas
cucumber	turnips	cabbage	potato
Jerusalem	winter squash	cauliflower	raw vegetables
artichokes	yams	celery	spinach
mushrooms	kale	cilantro	
okra	zucchini	corm, fresh	
pickled vegetables.			

Animal Foods (for non-vegetarians)

YES		AVOID/REDUCE	
chicken	sea food	beef	rabbit
lamb	turkey	pheasant	
pork			

DIET FOR REDUCING VATA IMBALANCE (CONTINUED)

Dairy

YES	AVOID/REDUCE
all dairy products, especially femented like yogurt, buttermilk and keifer	

Beans

made into a paste or pulse: chick peas (humus), mung beans, pink lentils	All beans should be avoided except for pulses (dal), green beans and tofu.

Oils

all oils, but best sesame oil and ghee, mayonnaise	com oil	mustard oil

Spices

all spices	clove	cayenne	nutmeg
anise	coriander	chilli	peppermint
asafoetida	cumin	juniperbery	sage
basil	fennel	mustard	turmeric
bay	garlic		
black pepper	ginger		

Reducing Imbalance by Diets

(small amts.)	onion		
caraway	salt		
cardamon	tarragon		
cinnamon	thyme		

Nuts and Seeds

all nuts   peanuts dry roasted

Sweeteners

sugar cane	molasses	raw honey	carob
products	rice syrup		

Beverages

hot herbal teas	1 small glass	cold drinks	black tea
warm rice milk	wine (no sulfites)	coffee	all other
	with meals		alcohol

DIET FOR REDUCING PITTA IMBALANCE

YES   **AVOID/REDUCE**

Grains

barley	wheat, rye	brown rice	millets
buckwheat	white rice	corn-yellow	yeasted breads
oat	(basmati)		
soda breads &	corn-blue		
pancakes			

Fruits

coconut	pomegranate		
cherries	sweet fruits	grapefruit	peaches
grapes	sweet oranges	lemon juice	persimmon
mango	sweet	limes	sour oranges
melons	pineapple	olives	sour pineapple
pear	sweet plums		

Vegetables

asparagus	okra	beets	onion
broccoli	peas	carrots	parsley

YES		AVOID/REDUCE	
brussels sprouts	potato	chard	pickles
	pumpkin	chillies	purple peppers
cabbage	steamed	eggplant	radish
cauliflower	onions(sweet)	garlic	spinach
celery	sweet potato	hot peppers	tomato
cucumber	turnips	mustard greens	white onions
green beans	zucchini		
mushrooms			

Dairy

YES		AVOID/REDUCE	
butter	milk	cheese	salty cheeses
cottage cheese	rice	cultured	sour cream
cream cheese	soybean ice	buttermilk	yogurt
ghee	cream	kefir	

Beans

YES	AVOID/REDUCE
most beans, especially mung. tofu, aduki, black chickpeas, soybeans,	lentils, especially red

SPICES

YES		AVOID/REDUCE	
cardamon	lemongrass	cayenne	nutmeg
cilantro	lemon skin	celery seeds	pepper
cinnamon	lotus seeds	clove	oregano
coriander	mint	fenugreek	rosemary
cumin	turmeric	ginger	sage, salt
fennel		mustard seed	all other spices

Nuts and Seeds

YES		AVOID/REDUCE	
best if	lotus seed	almonds	pine nuts

Reducing Imbalance by Diets

sprouted	sunflower	cashews	pumpkin
coconut	(best not in summer)	peanuts	sesame seeds

Sweeteners

maple syrup	stivia	in doderation	
rice syrup	barley	honey	white sugar
		molasses	

Beverages

cold drinks	soy milk	alcohol	hot drinks
		coffe, tea	

Best to avoid/reduce
fermented products
meat
salt

TOBACCO

Diet for Reducing Kapha Imbalance

YES   **AVOID/REDUCE**

Grains

basmati rice	rye	barley	wheat
buckwheat	roasted grains	brown rice	whiterice
corn		oats	millet

Fruits

apple	persimmon	banana	orange
cranberry	pomegranate	coconut	papaya
dried fruit	raisins	dates	pineapple
kiwi	strawberry	figs	prunes
pear		grapes	sweet fruits
		melons	

Vegetables

artichokes	green salads	cucumber	zucchini
asparagus	hot pepper	okra	sweet and
juicy			

beets	leafy greens	sweet potatoes
vegetables		
bitter melon	lettuce	tomatoes
bok choy	mushrooms	
broccoli	mustard greens	
cabbage	onions	
carrots	potatoes	
cauliflower	radish	
celery	spinach	
chilli	sprouts	
eggplant	squash	
green pepper	swiss chard	

Dairy

| goat milk | small amt. | most dairy products |
| ghee | unsalted buttermilk | |

Beans

| all beans: aduki, fava, kidney chickpeas lentils, lima | | tofu in extreme kapha humus |

YES   **AVOID/REDUCE**

Oils

(small amounts)		all others
almond	mustard	
canola	soy	
corn	sunflower	

Sweeteners

| small amount only, raw, uncooked honey | all other sweeteners |

Nuts and Seeds

best if sprouted flax seed	pumpkin seed sunflower	peanuts	all others

Animal Foods

(for non vegetarians)

fresh water fish rabbit	turkey (dark meat) venison	beef chicken lamb, pork	seafood fat, no fried or greasy food

Spices

all spices, especially garlic and ginger	pickles salt	vinegar

Beverages

almond milk coffee (cup/day) cranberry juice	ginger tea old wine, 1sm. glass w/meals tea	ice cold drinks

• • •

22

Food According to Property

The three body elements- Vata, Pitta and Kapha (air, fire and water)- when in balance (Tridosha) and harmony in the body promote health, if out of balance they are extremely harmful. Fot this reason one must follow the dietary system accordingly to try to keep the element in balance.

The categories of elements and tastes given on the following pages an essential guide to understanding how they can be enhanced or destroyed in different combination.

Quickly Digested Foods

Ginger, bitter gourd, sucking mango, mangosteen, carrot, rice, buttermilk, pomegranate, parwal, puffed rice, black pepper, masur, white radish, lemon, small aubergines, black salt (sanchal), rock salt (sindaiva), dry ginger, elephant foot (Indian yam), turmeric (haldi) asafoetida (heeng), apple, betelnut.

Hard to Digest Foods

Black gram (urad), chickpea, muth, tamarind, cucumber, Alphonso mango, sliced mango, unripe banana, yellow marrow, dates, wheat, tindoor, black-eye bean, watermelon, sesame seed, yoghurt, basundi, black grapes, popcorn, spinach, potatoes, almonds, sweet lemon, large aubergine, butter beans, string beans, sprouted beans (of any kind), dry vegetables, sugar cane juice, apple, betelnut.

Kapha Producing Foods

Black gram (urad), tamarind, mango juice, mango fruit, kokkum, sugar, gur (Indian brown sugar, or 'Jaggari') sesame seeds, milk, oranges, string beans, sprouted beans, dry vegetables, sugar cane juice, apples.

Pitta Producing Foods

Black gram (urad), tamarind, ripe cucumber, kokkum, gur, watermelon, sesame seed, unripe pomegranate, salt, large aubergine, butter beans, sprouted beans, dry vegetable, asafoetids (heeng).

Vata Producing Foods

Alphonso mango, gur (2nd class), rice sesame seeds, spinach, muth, honey, masoor, ripe white radish, beans of all kinds sprouted beans, dry vegetables.

Kapha Destroying Foods

Ginger, ripe tamarind, amla, bitter gourd, Alphonso mango, unripe banana, dates, carrots, chickpeas, buttermilk, water melon, pomegranate, Indian marrow, parwal, maize, honey, muth, puffed rice, black pepper, masoor, mustard seed, lemon, salt, butter beans, drumstick, rock salt, elephant, food, ginger powder, betelnut, haldi, asafoetida (heeng).

Pitta Destroying Foods

Amla, Cucumber, bitter gourd, Alphonso mango, mango pulp, unripe banana, yellow pumpkin, wheat, chickpea, milk, coconut, parwal, water, maize, sweet lemon, string beans, apple, drumstick, rock salt, betelnut, haldi.

Vata Destroying Foods

Black gram (urad), fresh ginger, tamarind, amla, mango juice, ripe mango, unripe banana, yellow marrow, dates, sugar, carrot, wheat, tindoor, buttermilk, ripe water melon, yogurt, pomegranate, milk, black grapes, oranges, coconut, parwal, sliced mango, almonds, fresh butter, salt, lemon, small aubergine, string beans, apple, rock salt, ginger powder, haldi, asafoetids (heeng).

Foods which are Cold

Amla, bitter gourd (karela), ripe mango, banana, dates, wheat, tindoor, butter oil (ghee), chickpea, rice, spinach, dals(split beans and peas), black grapes, coconut and coconut water, potatoes, maize, puffed rice, fresh butter, string beans, dry peas, sugarcane juice, apple, rock salt, betelnut.

Foods which are Hot

Fresh ginger, black gram Urad, tamarind, kokkum, carrots, tindoor, ripe melon, sesame seeds and oil, yogurt, parwal, white radish and its leaves, mustard seeds, salt, aubergine, ginger powder, haldi.

Foods which Increase the Digestive Power

Ginger, tamarind, small round bitter gourd, cucumber, ripe mango, kokkum, buttermilk, sesame seeds, spinach, oranges, coconut water, parwal, fresh butter, lemon, black salt, elephant foot, ginger powder, betelnut, haldi, asafoetids (heeng).

Foods which Prepare Stomach Contents for Correct Assimilation

Carrots, turia, parwal, puffed rice, white radish and its leaves, lemon, aubergine, drumsticks, haldi, asafoetida (heeng).

Foods which are Easily Digested and Help to Bind Other Foods in the Intestines

Ginger, cucumber, Alphonso mango, kokkum, carrot, yogurt, pomegranate, muth, masoor, ginger powder, all fruits.

Foods which Cause Drying in the Body

Tamarind, cucumber, Alphonso mango, chickpea, rice spinach, popcorn, potatoes, maize, honey, masoor, ripe radish, dried peas, elephant foot, betelnut, haldi.

Stimulating Foods

Black gram (urad), ginger, ripe mango, ripe banana, cabbage, yellow pumpkin, dates, basmati rice, jalebi, pomegranate, milk, Indian marrow, black grapes, coconut water, parwal, potatoes, almond, fresh butter, lapsi (cracked wheat) sweet lemon, vada from urad dal, small aubergine, shrikand, sugarcane juice, apple, ginger powder.

Food which increase Strength

Black gram (urad), ripe mango, ripe banana, coconut, dates, kitchadi, wheat, jalebi, sesame seeds, pomegranate, milk, basundi, potatoes, fresh butter, chapati, lapsi, urad dal vada, string beans.

Rejuvenating Foods Amla, Ghee, Triphala, Milk, Harade

Laxative Foods

Tamarind, gur, wheat, milk, black grapes, black-eye beans, sugarcane juice, harade.

FATTENING FOODS

Yellow pumpkin, ripe banana, sesame oil, basundi, black grapes, chapati, lapsi, urad dal vada, shrikand, sugarcane juice, apple.

FOODS BENEFICIAL TO THE HEART

Ginger, dates, old gur, milk, coconut water, parwal, black salt, ginger powder.

• • •

23

Food Combining

Helps Digestive System and Balancing of Food Code

F- fenugreek (methi)	L- lovage (ajwain)
G- garlic	M- mustard (rai)
H- heeng (asafoetida)	(FLM- whole seeds)

Vegetables	Spices
Potato and brinjal	FMH
Potato and cabbage	FMH
Potato and cauliflower	FMH
Potato and beans	FMH
Potato and peas	FMH
Potato and okra	FMH
Potato and onion	FMH
Potato and bitter gourd	MH
Dudhi (white marrow) & channa dal	FMH
Turia and mung dal	FMHG
Choli (runner bean) & cucumber	LH
Choli (runner bean) & brinjal	FMH
Choli (runner bean) & turia	FMH
Okra and cucumber	LH
Guvar (runner bean) & red pumpkin	LHG

Part – IV

24

Wheat Grass

Celebrated American dietician and grass-expert Dr. Urp Thomas has spent 50 valuable years of his life studying different types of grass. In the course of his study, he examined a large variety of grass types. At the end of his deep and long research he has reached a conclusion that, "Among all types of grass, wheat grass is the best of all. It supplies man with all the necessary nutrients. Only 1 kg. of wheat grass can supply nourishment that can be obtained from 23 kg. of carefully selected vegetables. Wheat grass juice is a complete food in itself and anybody can subsist on it alone for the whole of his life."

Besides chlorophyll wheat grass also contains many other nutritious substances. It contains almost all the minerals. Magnesium contained in it is helpful in activating about 30 enzymes in the body. It contains almost all the vitamins, barring vitamin D and vitamin B, Fresh juice of wheat grass contains a much higher amount of vitamin C compared to the fresh juice of mosambi or orange. 100 g. wheat grass contains 18,000 international units of vitamin- A. Vitamin E contained in it is beneficial for the heart, the blood-vessels and sexual efficiency. Many physicians consider vitamin %, (laetrile) contained in it to be an effective and the only remedy for curing cancer. It contains many enzymes and gastric juices which are beneficial to the digestive system in various ways. About 90 to 100 mg. chlorophyll can be obtained from 100 g. fresh wheat grass. Such chlorophyll is always active and of a high quality.

The chemical formation o'J'L' the wheat grass juice bears a close resemblance to the chemical formation of human blood. Both the liquids are alkaline. Both of them have the same pH. And that is why wheat grass juice is digested and absorbed quickly in the body. It mixes with the blood very soon and reaches out to every cell in the body.

It is a universally acknowledged fact that among all grains, wheat is the best grain for human consumption. It can be grown anywhere and is therefore easily available everywhere. While the information regarding other varieties of grass is not easily available. Some of the varieties of grass contain substances harmful to human beings. But the wheat grass is a familiar variety that is completely safe and contains no harmful substance. Wheat grass can be grown in any type of environment and during any season of the year.

Wheat grass contains a special property that enables it to paralyse toxic elements of the body or to eliminate them from the body.

1. Alfalfa contains some of the best medicinal pro-' parties; but it is difficult to grow it in the home as its roots spread deeper in the ground. Besides, after sowing the seeds, alfalfa takes longer time before its grass is ready for consumption. Its taste is also comparatively pungent.
2. The taste of barley grass is bitter. Not only children, but even elders find it unpalatable to take it for a long time.
3. Paddy grass is generally very dry. Very little juice can be extracted from it.

4. Palak leaves contain minerals in abundance but very little gastric juices. Some people develop diarrhoea after consuming it—and therefore they can't take it in a large quantity. Besides that, as it contains oxalates, people who are suffering from gall-bladder stone can't take it.
5. Other green-leaf vegetables such as dill leaves and fenugreek leaves also contain many medicinal properties; but their taste is generally unpalatable. And secondly, they are not easily available round the year.

Taking all these points into account, we can certainly state that wheat grass juice is safe, innocent, palatable and full of benevolent properties.

TECHNIQUE FOR GROWING WHEAT GRASS

Now let us discuss the technique for growing wheat grass :

SELECTING A POT

For growing wheat grass very big and deep pots are not required. Take seven pots measuring one square feet and having a depth of about three inches. Take only seven pots because after sowing, wheat grows to the desired height after 7 days. As a substitute of pots we can also use wooden boxes, lower half of earthen pots, baskets or big tins. If there is a compound or a backyard in the house, wheat can be sowed in small flower-beds or land basins.

SOIL AND MANURE

Very sticky earth is not desirable for growing wheat grass. Barring that, any other type of earth can be used for growing wheat grass. But do not use the earth in which some chemical - fertilizer has been mixed. It is necessary to add some manure to the earth in order that the, wheat grass may grow well and may acquire some more nutritious elements. In villages, natural manure of cow dung etc. is easily available but in cities where it is not easily available we can buy packets of ready-made compost from the market and use it. But chemical fertilizer should never be used.

QUALITY OF WHEAT

For growing wheat grass a better quality of wheat with big grains should be preferred. Wheat grass grown out of big grains is always broad and full of juice. About 100 g. wheat should be sown at a time. This quantity of wheat gives us about 100 g. wheat grass which in turn yields 4 to 6 oz. of wheat grass juice. This quantity of juice is sufficient per day for one patient.

Before sowing the wheat, they should be sprouted. For sprouting them, first soak them in water for about twelve hours. Then wrap them in a wet thick cloth and tie them tightly for about another twelve to fourteen hours. As a result of this process, they are sprouted well and shoots appear on them.

This procedure of sprouting the wheat prior to sowing them is a useful one. If the wheat are recently harvested or are rotten or have insects in them, they do not grow well. The procedure of sprouting reveals all such things before they are sown in the ground or in a pot. It also helps to anticipate the percentage of the wheat that would grow. While, if they are sowed without sprouting them, it is on the fourth or the fifth day that the picture about the result would be clear and sometimes all the labour soil, manure and other material may just be wasted. Besides that, the patient would not get the adequate quantity of the juice on the appointed day. After soaking them in water and keeping them tightly wrapped, if only 50% of the wheat appear sprouted, it would be easy to decide that double the quantity of wheat is required for sprouting and subsequent sowing. This would ensure an adequate yield in the required time schedule.

TECHNIQUE FOR GROWING WHEAT GRASS

Spread the sprouted wheat on the soil bed. Spread them in a such a way that the grains are close to one another and remain almost in touch with one another. Now cover the grains with a thin layer of earth. Then lemmu", sprinkle some water on it. Remember, water has to be sprinkled only, not to be poured over it. Overdosage of water spoils them altogether. If the water sprinkled on the wheat grass is not just ordinary water, but water treated with magnets it produces better results. Wheat grass not only grows very fast but also contains a higher amount of nutritious elements. This has been proved and verified through several experiments.

TECHNIQUE TO TREAT WATER WITH MAGNETS

Take a glass of water and a pair of powerful magnets (of about 2000 gauss each). Each magnet has two poles : North pole and South pole. Place the magnets on both the sides of the glass in such a way that the north pole remains on' one side and on the other remains the South pole. Put a lid on the glass and leave it in that position for about 12 to 15 hours, at the end of which the water is magnetised.

When the grass grows [Technique to treat water a bit high, give water with magnets) only once during 24 hours. But during summer it might be necessary to sprinkle water 2 or 3 times a day. For giving water to the plant, late afternoon or early evening is generally considered to be the right time.

See to it that the pots do not remain exposed to the sunlight for more than 3 to 4 hours during the daytime. When the sun is blazing in the afternoon, keep the pots under a shade.

Bear in mind that only one pot per day has to be prepared. Do not prepare all the seven pots at a time. Sow 100 g. wheat i.e in a pot on the first day. Thereafter, sow 100 g. wheat in a pot everyday for the succeeding six days. On the eighth day you'll find that the about 4 to 5 inches high wheat grass is ready in the first pot. So, on the eighth day, from that pot, cut the grass, with a pair of scissors, as close to the bottom as possible. Extract juice from the grass after washing it properly. Never pull out the grass from its very roots.

Do not allow wheat grass to grow higher than 4 to 5 inches as the proportion of chlorophyl and other nutritious. elements starts reducing from the leaves thereafter. Besides that their softness also reduces thereafter and as a result of that less juice can is obtained from the grass.

After cutting the grass, the earth from the pot should be spread over to allow it to dry in the sunlight. The same earth can be used after about 4 or 5 days. But before reusing it, add some fresh earth and manure.

Care of the pots and the growing wheat grass : It is necessary to protect the growing and fresh and tender wheat grass from insects, birds and rodents.

Use wooden racks to protect the wheat grass from, insects, birds and rodents. Place the pots on the shelves of a wood rack and then cover the rack with a wire network or meshes, so as to allow the plants to get adequate air and sunlight. Wrap the legs of the rack with cloth pieces: soaked in castor oil or keep them in small vessels filled with water so as to keep ants and other insects off the wooden rack.

It is likely that sometimes during summer wheat grass may not grow well due to heat. So, under such circumstances sow maize seeds instead of wheat and extract the juice of maize grass. Maize grass is only slightly inferior to the wheat grass in quality and medicinal properties.

Proper Dosage and Timings

In the beginning restrict the intake of wheat grass or its juice dosage. Increase the intake of the dosage gradually. In an ordinary illness or for a common ailment 100 g. wheat grass or 100 mi. juice per day is an adequate dosage. But those who are suffering from some serious or chronic disease should start with 25 to 50 mi. per day and gradually raise the dosage so as to reach a quantity of 250 to 300 mi. per day.

Even after the disease is cured, it is advisable to continue to take 50 mi. juice everyday in order to maintain proper health. Any normal, healthy person can also take this quantity of the juice to maintain his good health and avoid illness.

If the dosage or intake is kept high from the beginning, then it is likely in some cases that the patient may -complain of nausea, vomiting sensation, cold, diarrhoea or fever or similar other troubles. So, keep the dosage or intake low in the beginning and raise it gradually. But do not get panicky even if the above-listed complains arise. Dilute the juice before taking it. And if the complaints persist beyond two or three days, stop taking the wheat grass or its juice for a couple of days and resume it only after the complains have subsided.

Proper timings for taking the juice : It is advisable to take the juice early in the morning on an empty stomach. After taking the wheat grass or its juice, do not eat or drink anything for about half an hour. The juice gets absorbed in the intestines within half an hour after it is taken. Those who find it inconvenient to take it in the early morning can take it at any time during the day when the stomach is empty. But those who wish to obtain the gains of both the methods of wheat grass intake should take the juice in the morning only, and should chew the wheat grass at any other convenient hour or at short convenient intervals during the day.

NATURAL RESISTANCE POWER

We, the Indians believe that health would automatically remain normal and in case there is any trouble we can always take drugs to cure any ailment. Most of us are apathetic to matters of health. Generally we are indifferent and inactive about maintaining good health. We hardly ever give any serious thought to our health preservation needs. In modern times, ignorance about the health perhaps exceeds our ignorance on any other subject.

In reality, ailments or sickness are not absolutely inevitable. If our natural resistance power is strong enough, no disease would dare to attack us. If we do not disrupt the process of natural resistance, it would see us through hale and hearty till the end of our life. No germs of disease can affect a healthy man with powerful natural resistance.

Dr. Thomas Powell of California who died at the age of 80 had introduced, in his body, numerous bacteria and viruses. He had thrown an open challenge to his physician friends that they could introduce in- his body any number of bacteria and viruses, but, he was sure, they would not adversely affect his health in any way. To take the wind out of his challenge many virologists made efforts for a number of years. Germs of deadly diseases like plague, cholera etc. were introduced in his body through food as well as through injections. Germs of diphtheria were stuffed several times into a wound in his throat after fraying that portion over and over again. Nevertheless, no infection of any germs could affect Dr. Powell in any way.

The secret of such a powerful natural resistance is very simple. With the progress in civilization man increasing kept on violating the laws of Nature and the rate incidence of diseases also rose commensurate with moving away from the Nature. In ancient times physician were aware of the healing power of Nature. They knew it well that it is the Nature, and not the physician that really cures a patient. The word 'physician' is derived from the Greek word 'physis' (meaning : Nature). Dr. Swinburne Clymer, M. D. says : "I never make a claim that I have cured a patient. It is the Nature that cure him. I am only an instrument in that process."

Head of the Department of Pharmacology in Saskech van University of Canada, Dr. Wendell Mcleod appeal to man to return to Nature and says, "In fact we should have faith in the natural resistance power and Nature healing power. But we are leaning more and more towards the use of drugs and medicines."

Professor in Preventive Medicine at the Chicago University in Loyala Prof. Herbert Rutner says, "By not giving Nature an opportunity (to cure us) we are unduly haste. We start taking patent drugs even at the slightest symptom of an ordinary illness. The natural resistance power of a body can cure most of our illnesses and no medical inter vention is required for them."

It is not proper to treat this 'natural resistance power of our body as a mere creation of our imagination. D Hans Selye, Director of Experimental Medicine and Surgej at the Montreal University has proved its existence by conducting several experiments. He calls it 'Adoptation Energy'. This energy helps man in resisting physical, chemical and psychological tension and for remaining healthy and fit.

• • •

25

Medicinal Properties of Barley / Maize / Rice / Wheat

NATURAL BENEFITS AND MEDICINAL POPERTIES OF BARLEY

Barley has many medicinal virtues. Pearled barley, which is the form the grain is largely eaten and consumed as a food by invalids. The malt prepared from barley is used in the preparation of malt extract for the incorporation in the diet of the infant and the invalid.

The partially germinated and dried grain is the source of malt extract which is more nutritious than the uninalted barley. Malt extract consists chiefly of dextrin and malt sugar and contains the ferment diastase enzyme which is developed during the malting process. This ferment diastase possesses the power of converting starch into dextrin and sugar, thus assisting in the digestive of starchy or farinaceous foods.

NATURAL BENEFITS AND MEDICINAL PROPERTIES OF MAIZE

The bread made from the maize flour is nutritious and palatable. It can be digested without difficulty. Taken at intervals, this bread helps to keep the colon clean. The dextrose produced from maize is used extensively in medicine.

NATURAL BENEFITS AND MEDICINAL PROPERTIES OF RICE

Rice has always been considered a magical healer in the East. it was originally believed to have medicinal values that could restore tranquility and peace to those who were easily upset. It has been mentioned in easily Oriental writings that natural whole grain brown rice is a perfect healing food. In the ancient literature of Thailand, Burma, Malaya and Indo-China rice is mentioned as a source of health. It was also revered as a food of divine health and used in religious offerings.

Modern researches have confirmed the beliefs of ancient oriental folk physicians that the eating of brown rice is a source of serenity and tranquility. It has been shown to contain all the elements needed for the maintenance of good health.

Rice is about 98 per cent digestible. It is one of the most easily and quickly digested of all foods-being fully digested-in an hour. Rice starch is different from other grain starches as it contains 100 per cent amylopectin which is most completely and rapidly digested grain starch. This makes rice in ideal health food for those who seek speedy and healthy assimilation.

NATURAL BENEFITS AND MEDICINAL PROPERTIES OF WHEAT

The wheat, as produced by nature, contains several medicinal virtues. Every part of the whole wheat grain supplies elements needed by the human body. Starch and gluten-in wheat provide heat and energy; the inner bran coats, phosphates and other mineral salts; the outer bran, the much-needed roughage the indigestable portion which helps easy movement of bowels; the germ, vitamins B and E; and protein of wheat helps build and repair muscular tissue. The wheat germ, which is removed in the process of refining, is also rich in essential vitamin E, the lack of which can lead to heart disease. The loss of vitamins and minerals in the refined wheat flour has led to widespread prevalence of constipation and other digestive disturbances and nutritional disorders. The whole wheat, which includes bran and wheat germ, therefore, provides protection against diseases such as constipation, ischaernic, heart disease, disease of the colon called diverticulum, appendicitis, obesity and diabetes.

• • •

26

Medicinal Properties of Honey / Milk / Sugarcane / Curd

Honey is one of the finest sources of heat and energy. Energy is generated mainly by the carbohydrate foods and honey is one of the most easily digested form of carbohydrates. It enters directly into the bloodstream because of its dextrine content and this provides almost instantaneous energy. It is a boon to those with weak digestion. All organs in the body respond favourably when honey is eaten. The famous Roman physician, Galen has described honey as an all purpose medicine for all types of diseases. It is now used as a Medicinal and preventive for several ailments.

One spoon of fresh honey-mixed with the juice of half a lemon in a glass of lukewarm water and taken first thing in the morning, is an effective remedy for constipation and hyperacidity. Fasting on this honey-lemon juice water is highly beneficial in the treatment of obesity without loss of energy and appetite.

A mixture of honey and alcohol growth of hair it is said that Japanese geistia giris, luxuriant hair, mix several tablespoonful of honey with alcohol, stirring them together. They massage this mixture onto the scalp, allow it to remain there for two hours and then wash or rinse with shampoo thoroughly. It is said that regular use of this honey-alcohol mixture stimulates the hair follicles to grow into luxuriant tresse.

Milk

According to Charaka, the great author of the Indian system of medicine, milk increases strength, improves memory, removes exhaustion, maintains strength and promotes long life. Experiments conducted in modern times have, amply coroborated this opinion of Charaka.

Milk is the only article of diet which is well accepted as a wholesome food for persons of all ages, from infancy to old age. It is of special value in feeding infants, toddlers, growing children and expectant and nursing mothers. It is also recommended as a wholesome food for invalids.

Under Weight

Milk diet is highly beneficial in the treatment of thinness. If one is considerably below the normal weight, the gain will be from three to five pounds a week, depending upon the quantity of milk consumed. The body gradually fills out. The eyes become clear and bright and the complexion assumes a healthy colour. The assimilative organs gain renewed energy and power and the gain in the weight is permanent.

Sugarcane

Sugarcane juice has many medicinal properties. It strengthens the stomach, kidneys, heart, eyes, brain and sex organs.

Fevers

The juice is beneficial in fevers. In febrile disorders which causes fever, when there is great protein loss, liberal intake of sugarcane juice supplies the body with necessary protein and other food elements.

Jaundice

Mixed with lime juice, it can hasten recovery from jaundice. It is, however, very essential that the juice, must be clean, preferably prepared at home. Resistance is low in hepatitis and any infected beverage could make matters worse.

Weak Teeth

The juice sucked from the sugarcane can prove highly valuable in case of weak teeth due to lack of proper exercise resulting from excessive use of soft foods. It gives a form of exercise to the teeth and makes them strong. It also keeps the teeth clean and increases their life.

Thinness

Sugarcane juice is a fattening food. It is thus an effective remedy for thinness. Rapid pin in weight can be achieved by its regular use.

Eye Disorders

The dew which collects on the long leaves of sugarcane is useful in several eye disorders. When instilled in the eyes, it is an effective medicine in defective vision, cataract, conjunctivitis, burning of the eyes and eye-strain after excessive reading.

Genito-urinary Disorders

Sugarcane is very useful in scanty urination. It keeps the urinary flow clear and helps the kidneys to perform their functions properly. It is also valuable in burning micturation due to high acidity, gonorrhoea, enlarged prostate, cyctitis and nepthritis. For better results, it should be mixed with lime juice, ginger juice and coconut water.

NATURAL BENEFITS AND MEDICINAL PROPERTIES OF CURD

Although curd has a nutritive content similar to fresh milk, it has extensive special values for therapeutic purposes. During the process of making curd, bacteria convert milk into curd and predigest milk protein. These bacteria then inhibit the growth of hostile or illness-causing bacteria inside the intestinal tract and promote beneficial bacteria needed for digestion. These friendly bacteria facilitate the absorption of minerals and aid in the synthesis of vitamins of B group. Buttermilk, which has same nutritive and Medicinal value as curd, is prepared by churning curd and adding some water, removing the fat in the form of butter.

Curd is also considered one of the best aids to natural good looks. It supplies the nerves and the skin with healthy ingredients and counteracts the ill-effects of exposure to the scorching sun. The bacteria in curd make the skin soft and glowing. Curd mixed with orange or lemon juice is a good face cleanser. It supplies moisture to the skin and fruit juice provides the essential vitamin C. One tablespoonful of juice should be mixed in one cup of curd. This should be applied to face and neck and allowed to dry for 15 minutes. It should then be wiped of with a soft tissue and washed with water.

A mixture of oatmeal flour and yogurt has been found effective in making the skin fairer and softer. This mixture should be kept on the facial skin for 15 to 20 minutes and then washed off with warm water. For pimples, a paste of curd and Bengal gram flour or besan should be applied on the face and then washed off.

Curd is also considered valuable in conditioning the hair. It makes the hair soft, healthy and strong. Curd should be massaged right into the roots of the hair before being washed off. Dandruff can be removed by massaging one's hair for half an hour with curd which has been kept in the open for three days.

• • •

27

Juices for Healthy Life

Make fruit and juice an essential part of your daily diet-in their natural unprocessed form.

Age is no bar for fruits and juice. However, old and young you are, you must make it a habit to have a glass or two of fresh juice daily. Continuous use of fresh and processed fruits coupled with other intoxicants shatters good health and all toxins generated by the regular use of such foods must be purged out of the system-something that can be effectively done by drinking juices. Besides, they are full of nutritive value and restore lost health, vigour and vitality and make your skin glow like never before.

Juice is capable of correcting metabolism and helps immensely in repairing torn out, fatigued and exhausted tissues.

Several diseases such as diabetes, digestion related disorders (flatulence, diarrhoea, gastritis, gastralgia colic, acidity, nausea, vomiting), asthma and other respiratory disorders and other diseases occur primarily because of the apparent indiscreet use of food. Most often, fat-enriched food, an imbalance in protein-carbohydrate intake, lack of water intake and irregular dietary habits act as catalysts for food related disorders. Green vegetables and fruits, either in their raw form or as juice should be included in your regular diet. But the quantity differs for people of different ages. Certain fruits and vegetables however, must be avoided for certain ailments.

In winters, carrot juice mixed with spinach and lemon and little ginger is very beneficial. But if a person is prone to colds, avoid lemon.

SOME TIPS ON JUICING

- Buy only the best fruits.
- Make sure fruits have not been artificially ripened and are free from the harmful effects of pesticides and other chemicals. Fruits ripened by carbide will be more harmful and may cause digestive and other physical disorders.
- Vegetables should be fresh. If they are green and leafy, the leaves should be bright green and not limp.
- Always make it a habit to wash all vegetables and fruits with fresh water, before use and to discard all decayed portions.
- Juice once extracted should be drunk without delay. Do not store in the refrigerator.
- Wash the juicer before and after use promptly to avoid contamination.
- In pregnancy or severe ailments 250 to 350 ml of fruit juice or vegetable juice should be taken twice regularly.

Most of the dreaded diseases like diabetes, cancer, asthma, most digestion-related disorders (like flutulence, diarrhoea, gastralgia, colic, acidity, nausea, vomiting etc.) and other respiratory diseases owe their causation to wrong and indiscreet use of foods. Very often imbalanced, fat-enriched, imbalance in protein-carbohydrate intake, lack of water intake are often held as attributes of food-related disorders.

JUICE FOR INFANTS

Digestive system of an infant is very sensitive because he is fed on mother's milk or on tinned milk. No solids are given to an infant upto the age of six months, for obvious reasons. After six months, juice of Sweet Lime, Orange or grapes or meshed Banana can be and is generally given, of course in addition to usual intake of milk and cereals. Care must be taken to ensure that any kind of juice, to which the infant resists and shows any disinclination or dislike (or still worse, if he vomits) should never be forced upon the infant. It is advisable that fruit should be slightly luke warmed to infant's tolerance, in the afternoon or evening. Never force any food item upon an infant if he shows dislike.

JUICE FOR GROWING CHILDREN

As it is well known, from 5 to 12 years, a child embarks upon growth stage and, his body requires plenty of repeated servings of essential food nutrients. Young ones must be given plenty of fresh green vegetable and fruit juices-once, at least in the afternoon (just an hour or so prior to lunch) and once in the evening, when they return after playing. Timings can be adjusted as per individual suitability and need. It is a myth that costlier fruits and vegetables carry more nutrients. In fact, other less costly ones are equally capable of giving similar, if not better, results.

JUICE FOR THE ADOLESCENT & GROWN UP YOUNG PEOPLE

From 12 years onwards a young one enters the age which shows changes and expansion of various organs. This is rightly called a 'Critical Stage' because changes noticed and experienced baffle the young ones and their food habits, attitude, likes and dislikes undergo a change. It is particularly true of young girls, having their first menstrual flow. Let the young person be made aware of physical changes and consequences flowing therefrom.

In this age group, plenty of raw and fresh fruits and vegetables, and advise, include the young one to prefer natural eatables to canned, fried foods, canned or tinned/bottled juices and soft drinks and foods. They benefit none but the sellers.

Adolescents and grown-ups must have atleast a glass of fresh juice, either of fruits or vegetables, in the afternoon or as a substitute with supper. During both principal meals, they must take leafy and green vegetables or juice or soup or such items. If that is not feasible, they must have the same in raw but natural form. Those, who have impacted and constipated bowels should, as a matter of routine, take lemon juice in lukewarm glassful water and those whose bowels are sensitive should take juice of Stone Apple (Aegle Marmelos) or Papaya-once in the morning and once in the evening or at bed time and such persons should avoid taking spinach (Palak), lady-finger (Bhindi)-rather any vegetable/fruit which abound in starch and iron content.

JUICE FOR PREGNANT LADIES

Digestion of a pregnant woman is generally impaired due to lack of physical movement and proper/suitable exercise. Keeping this fact in view, it has to be stressed that she should avoid all heavy, starchy, fatty, fried and spicy food. Instead, the emphasis should be laid on calorie based diet suiting an individual's requirements. Liquified diet like fruit and vegetable juices, milk, pulses etc. should be preferred. As far as possible meat based diet should be avoided, still better if totally eliminated. A pregnant mother's diet is partaken by the foetus in her womb, hence food should almost be doubled. She has to take care of her own health as also of her off-spring's development aspect.

Keeping aforesaid points in view a pregnant lady should take plenty of juices, extracted from oranges, lime, apples, grapes, guava, water-melons, musk-melons, leechis and all such green vegetables from which juice could be extracted. 250-350 ml. of juice of fruits/vegetable should be taken at least twice daily- before or after meals. Mango-shake is an excellent nutrient as it is rich in many nutrients. Those, who do not or cannot take juice, should take them in their raw form.

JUICE FOR AGED PERSONS

In old age, many physical problems like, obesity, diabetes, hypertension, gout, cough and cold, asthma, stiff and painful joints and other allied disorders, respiratory problems and many other diseases continue to torture and torment the aged, leading to mental and physical inactivity and inertia. Major problem lies in weak digestion, reduced food intake, lack of exercise. It is very difficult to recommend a particular type of juice therapy for each and individual person separately. Problem arises because a particular juice extract may be beneficial to one, but not to the other.

Keeping infirmities and limitations of the old and the aged, easily digestible fruits like Grapes, Lime, Mangoes, Leechis, Water enriched fruits, Tomatoes, Spinach, Mint, Garlic, Coriander, Lemon, Beet and Leafy vegetables, should be used for juicing purposes. One has to be rather decisive what suits a person and what not. Only such vegetables/fruits or their juices should be used which do not create any health hazard or still worse do not aggravate already existing ailments. Meat diet should never be used. Dry fruits should also be rarely used, especially which are rich in oily contents. Disease based and need-based juice diet should always be preferred to starchy, fatty, greasy, spicy, fried and meat diet. It should always be borne in mind that main criterion should be towards consumption of light, juicy, liquids which respond to physical needs, correct metabolism and improve general well-being. A Wigmore is the authority on Juice-Therapy, who has treated thousands of patients suffering from incurable ailments, throughout the world.

THERAPEUTIC BENEFITS OF FRESH JUICES

Human beings get well on live juices when nothing else seems to work. This is what Max Gerson, M.D., found when he put his cancer patients on a juicy therapy regimen. His 'gentle' treatment of cancer is described in detail in his book, "A Cancer Therapy : Results of Fifty Cases". The fifty people he discusses all covered from cancer through his natural treatments.

• • •

28

Magic of Water

An old Japanese gentleman who enjoyed perfect health, was once met by a curious professor. When asked about the secret of his robust constitution, the old man explained that it was thanks to the water Wonder. He went on to tell in detail about his sickly youth, when he was bed-ridden, with impaired intestines, for almost ten years. When all the modes of treatment failed to bring even partial relief from his sickness, he was told it was impossible to get a cure. One of the physicians who treated him, however, suggested a specific type of water treatment as a last resort.

The effect of the treatment was felt on the very first day and his appetite was restored, his digestion improved and within a few days he was cured of his chronic disease. It might have been a coincidence that the treatment he underwent all those years showed results only after this simple water treatment. So impressed with this treatment was he, that he tried it on the members of his family who were suffering from various illnesses ranging from brain fever to obesity and achieved positive results.

WHAT IS THE WATER MAGIC?

The process is as follows :- Go to sleep three hours after a fairly early dinner around 7.00 p.m. Strictly do not eat or drink anything after that. Rise early from bed the next morning, do not wash your face and mouth as you do normally. Sit comfortably and drink six glasses of pure water at a stretch. If you find difficulty in doing so, pause a while after two or three glasses and continue. For the next 20 minutes walk briskly or do some exercise. Within twenty minutes to half an hour, urge to pass urine will be great and you will pass urine in large quantities quite frequently. Some may bring out the morbid waste through vomiting. Passing of stools will be easy and complete. It will facilitate the expulsion of the accumulated waste matter very effectively and leave you fresh.

• • •

29

Medicinal Properties of Pulses / Seeds / Nuts

SOYABEAN

Soyabean milk is at par in importance with cow's milk in feeding children. Investigation's have shown that 90 per cent of the soyabean protein is absorbed in the body and 95 to 100 percent of the milk is digested. Soyabean milk is very helpful in maintaining.intestinal health. The soyabean curd is a health food par excellence. It is better than soyabean milk in taste and aroma and it very much resembles the dairy curd The curd is prepared by allowing the milk to cool, then seeded with a small quantity of cow's milk curd or soyabean milk curd and allowed to remain for 12 hours to set. Its regular use will help maintain the intestinal health, prevent diseases arising from defective digestion and retard the ageing process.

One of the chief uses of soyabeans is as a source of lecithin, which is a great natural emulsifier. Lecithia, as is well known helps disperse deposits of fatty materials and cholesterol in certain vital organs. It is rich in substances which are important for the proper functioning of all living cells in the body. It is also an important component around brain and cells. Lecithin is so abundant in soyabeans that most of the lecithin used commercially comes from them.

Diabetes

Soyabean contains a fairly-large amount of carbohydrate but there is little or no starch in it. It is, therefore, regarded as a very suitable food for diabetic patient. Its carbohydrate produces heat and energy in the body without causing sugar to appear in the urine.

Skin Disorders

The soyabean is regarded as a valuable food remedy in eczema and other skin affections. It renders unnecessary the use of animal protein, that is, meat, eggs and milk and thus reduces the' inflammatory activities in the skin and is free from the tendency to produce sensitivity or allergic reactions which so frequently attend the users of all animal proteins. When soyabean is taken liberally, the intense itching diminishes almost immediately and disappears completely after a few days. Improvement in skin health presumably occurs due to its lecithin content a natural emulsifier which helps disperse fatty deposits and cholesterol from vital organs.'

Anaemia

Soyabean, being rich in iron, has been found beneficial in the treatment of anaemia. As, however, the anaemic patients suffer from weak digestion, it should be given to them in a very light form which may be easily digested.

Uses

Soyabeans are used in other forms such as flour, green beans, sprouts and oil. The soya flour is one of the most widely used products of soyabean. In the West, the soyabean flour industry has grown to immense proportions. The soya flour is prepared by first roasting the soyabeans and removing their coatings. They are then turned into powder. It is by far more nutritious than the wheat flour. It contains 15 times as much calcium, seven times as much phosphorus, 10 times as much iron, 10 times as much thiamine and nine times as much riboflavin as wheat flour.

PRECAUTIONS

Soyabean contains a bitter substance which can be removed by soaking soyabean in six cupfuls of warm water containing half a teaspoon of sodium bicarbonate for 10 minutes. The process also removes the colouring matter from soyabean. Soyabeans contains a factor which inhibits the action of the digestive enzyme trypsin. This factor can be destroyed by heating.

GRAM (CHANA)

It is very nutritive. Regular intake of Chana imparts a lot of physical vigour and strength to the muscles and all parts of the body.

Chana is invigorating, purifier of blood, digestive, antibilleous and anti phlegm, atic pyretuci, pain-killer, germicidal, and very effective in cold and cough.

NOTE

(i) Chana should be taken along with its husk for that helps in assimilating full protein in the body.

(ii) Excessive intake of Besan should be avoided as it causes indigestion and diarrhoea.

(iii) Water should not be taken just after eating chanas, chapatis, bun etc. for the gram flour will form a paste with water and that will cause constipation and indigestion.

MEDICINAL PROPERTIES

GENERAL TONIC

(i) Sprouted Chanas (Soak chanas for 1 day in summers & 2 days in winters. Hang them for 2 days in a wet cloth and they are sprouted) with grated ginger, little sendha Namak, Black pepper and lemon-juice sprinkled on it is an ideal breakfast. This is very rich in Vitamin C and gives strength and energy to the entire body.

(ii) Taking 200 gms. milk (in which 20 gms. of chana or 40 gms. of chane

(iii) Dal had been soaked over night in the breakfast after chewing finely the soaked chanas or chane ki dal-gives lot of stamina.

(iii) Taking Chutney of green gram-strengthens bones and muscles of the body.

(iv) Taking chanas regularly makes the man's muscles very strong and free from problems like early ejaculation or lack of sexual power.

ANAEMIA

Taking sprouted chanas in breakfast cures anaemia.

ARTHRITIS

Taking boiled grams with honey in the morning makes the joints supple.

HEART TROUBLE

Taking roasted Chana or soaked black Chana is very useful for heart patients.

Indigestion and Stomach Problem

(i) Taking sprouted Chana in the morning stimulates appetite.

(ii) Taking Raita of Bundi (made from ground gram) with little roasted Jeerapowder, dry Pudina powder with food eliminates all digestive problems.

(iii) Taking 10-15 gms. juice of soft fresh leaves of Chana plant eliminates gases.

Constipation

Eating Chana (soaked overnight) in the morning with ground Jeera and Sonth sprinkled on it and also drinking the water (in which Chana was soaked) eliminates constipation.

Cold

(i) Taking milk after eating roasted chana before going to bed- eliminates the phlegm. and clears the wind pipe.

(ii) Smelling the roasted hot-chana (tied in a potil) stops running nose.

(iii) Eating roasted chanas helps in releasing trapped phlegm..

(iv) Eating thick chapati of chana choker flour with little Ajwain, Heeng, black-pepper powder-cooked on slow fire with thin dal helps in curing chronic cold.

Stones

(i) Taking Chana ki Dal Soaked overnight with honey helps in breaking the stones in bladder, kidney and throwing them out.

(ii) Drinking water of Black Chana and wheat (which have been soaked overnight and boiled in the morning) is also very useful.

(iii) Eating chapatis made of ground chana and wheat regularly is useful in dissolving and throwing out of stones.

Asthma

(i) Taking 40-50 gms. of roasted chanas in the evening-followed with hot milk-clears the phlegm in the bronchial chords.

(ii) Eating whole gram Parantha or Rotis with pieces of onion stuffed in it followed by hot milk eliminates excessive phlegm. in the respiratory system.

Hoarse Voice

(i) Eating crushed black chana (soaked over night) boiled in 250 gms. milk with 2 tsp. of honey-slowly helps in de-straining the vocalchords and cures hoarse voice.

Hair

Applying a solution of Besan with water on the hair for 10-15 minutes and then washing with lukewarm water 'eliminates dryness of the hair, makes them soft and lustrous and checks dandruff.

Skin-Care

(i) Washing the face with around chana (Besan)-removes spots and freckles

(ii) Applying the paste of Besan with mustard oil-on the affected part softly and gradually rubbing it off the skin after 30-40 minutes-clears the skin, improves the complexion, removes the white patches (especially if they are due to dryness in winter season).

(iii) Applying a paste of Besan with milk or curd-on the face for half an hour-improves the complexion and imparts glow.

ITCHING SKIN AILMENTS

(i) Eating ground chana roti without salt, with or without ghee regularly-for 2 months eliminates blood impurities, itching and cures all skin problems.

(ii) Taking sprouted gram early in the morning and also the water in which they were soaked-eliminates all blood impurities.

(iii) Applying a smooth paste of gram plant mixed with mustard oil on the body half an hour before bath-eliminates itching sensation of the body.

(iv) Taking chutney made, of gram plant purifies the skin and gives energy.

LEUCODERMA

(i) Eating ground chana chapati is very useful.

(ii) Sprouted chanas (Soak 20 gm. chana with 10 gm. at Triphala, Harar, Bahar, Amla-in 125 gm. water and then keep it for 24 hours for sprouting) regularly helps in curing leucoderma.

URTICARIA

(i) Eating Besan Laddus with black-pepper sprinkled on it- cures unicaria.

(ii) Taking Besan Bundi Raita with black-pepper and sugar- cures urticaria.

PAIN

Massaging the affected part of the body with Besan eliminates pain.

VOMITING

(i) Taking water only in which chana has been soaked, helps in curing vomiting.

(ii) Taking Sattu of chana with water and sugar (Sattu by grinding roasted gram and barley) controls vomiting during pregnancy.

DIARRHOEA

Taking the water of chana husk (Soaked for half an hour. Keep it on cloth and have the oozed out water) frequently stops loose motions.

LEUCORRHOEA

Eating ground roasted chana with jaggery followed by drinking milk with pure ghee-helps in curing leucorrhoea.

PILES

Eating slightly hot roasted chana helps in curing piles.

JAUNDICE

Taking chana ki dal soaked overnight with gur in equal quantity for 3-4 days and also drinking the same water (in which dal was soaked) when thirsty-helps in eliminating jaundice.

POLYRIA

(i) Taking little gur after eating 10 gm. roasted chanas-regularly checks tendency of frequent urinating.
(ii) Roasted chana taken without water also checks polyria.

ABORTION, DELIVERY ETC.

(i) Taking decoction of Black Chana (by boiling 200 gms. chana in 400 gms. water till the water is reduced to half) regularly after conception is preventive against abortion.
(ii) Taking 10 gms. barley gram ground powder with little ground Black Til and Sugar followed by a glass of hot milk

after the conception regularly is also very useful to prevent abortion.

(iii) Chapatis made of ground whole gram and moth (a variety of pulse) with lunch and dinner-cleans the insides of the ovaries after delivery or abortion.

INCREASE IN MOTHER'S MILK

(i) Taking the boiled milk (in which Kabuli Chana has been soaked overnight) after chewing the chanas regularly helps the mother to have adequate milk in the breasts.

(ii) Chana (with husk) with honey or sugar also is useful.

DIABETES

(i) Taking Black Chana (soaked in milk overnight) eliminates sugar.

(ii) Chapatis of ground gram mixed with ground barley of only Besan in lunch and dinner cures diabetes.

WORMS

Taking Chana soaked overnight in vinegar in breakfast with little salt and onion pieces throws the worms out. (Caution-any amount of water can be taken but nothing solid in breakfast and lunch).

SEMEN

(i) Taking roasted chana or soaked chana with almonds (in the same proportion) followed by drinking milk, thickens the semen.

(ii) Soaked chane ki dal in the morning and at night with or without sugarcandy strengthens and enhances sexual potency.

Eye-Trouble

(i) Eating freshly roasted chana or soaked chanas gives relief to the tired and swollen eyes.
(ii) Taking fresh leaves of the Chana plant-is good for enhancing eye-sight.
(iii) Chane-ka-Saag with butter is also good for eyes.
(iv) Binding the freshly roasted chana in a potli-to foment the eyes and putting drop of rose-water reduces redness, pain and burning sensation in the eyes.

Green Gram

Cooked dal of green gram is a very digestive food for invalid and sick persons. Its regular use during childhood, pregnancy and lactation helps one to get the required nutrition and promote health. It is an aperient i.e. a laxative, when given in large quantities. The soup made from it is the best article of diet after recovery from acute illness.

Applied in the form of powder, it is said to be useful in relieving the heat or burning of the eyes. A poultice of this powder is useful for checking secretion of milk and reducing distention of the mammary glands.

Fevers

Water in which green grains are soaked is an excellent medicine during cholera, measles, chicken-pox, small-pox, typhoid and all types of fevers. It can be given in a small quantity, even during acute phase of appendicitis.

Beauty-Aid

Flour of the green gram is an excellent detergent and can be used as a substitute for soap. It removes the dirt and does not cause any skin irritation. Its application over the face bleaches the colour and gives good complexion. Black gram flour is also used for washing the hair with green gram paste to lengthen hair and prevent dandruff.

Pigeon pea

The pigeon pea is easily digested and therefore suitable for invalids. It has many medicinal properties. It relieves inflammation of internal organs. However, excessive use of pigeon pea causes hyper-acidity and wind in the intestines. Therefore, it is forbidden in gastric ulcer and heart diseases.

Jaundice

The expressed juice of the leaves given, with a little salt, is highly beneficial in the treatment of jaundice. 60ml of this juice should be taken daily in this condition.

Checking Breast Milk Secretion

The pulse and leaves ground into a paste, warmed and applied over the mamma, has the effect of checking the secretion of breast milk.

Inflammation

The leaves of the plant are effective in all inflammatory conditions. A poultice made with the seeds will also reduce swelling.

Piles

Paste of the levies, mixed with a teaspoonful of paste of neem leaves, is highly beneficial in the treatment of piles and itching in the anus. It should be taken once daily for a week.

Baldness

A fine paste made of this pulse is highly useful in bald patches It should be applied regularly.

• • •

General & Medicinal Properties of Fruits

Fruits are one of the oldest forms of food known to man. Fresh and dry fruits are the natural staple food of man. They contain substantial quantities of essential nutrients in a rational proportion. They are excellent sources of minerals, vitamins and enzymes. They are easily digested and exercise a cleaning effect on the blood and the digestive tract. Persons on this natural diet will always enjoy good health. Fresh and dry fruits are thus not only a good food but also a good medicine.

FRUITS

Fruits have highly beneficial effect on this human system. The main physiological actions of fruits are as follows:

HYDRATING EFFECT

Taking of fruits or fruit juice is the most pleasant way of hydrating the organism. The water absorbed by sick persons in this manner has an added advantage of supplying sugar and minerals at the same time.

DIURETIC EFFECT

Clinical observations have shown that potassium, magnesium and sodium contents of the fruit act as a diuretic and diuresis frequency of urination is considerably increased when fruits and fruit juice are taken. They lower the urine density and thereby accelerate the elimination of nitrogenous waste and chlorides.

Alkalinising Effect

The organic acids of the salts in fruits produce alkaline carbonates, when transformed within the organism, which alkalini the fluids. All fruits promote intestinal elimination. This keeps the body free from toxic wastes which creep into the blood from an overloading, sluggish intestinal tract.

Mineralising Effect

Fruits furnish minerals to the body. Dried fruits such as apricots, raisins and dates are rich in calcium and iron. These minerals are essential for strong bones and good blood respectively.

Laxative Effect

The fibrous matter in fruits, cellulose aids in the smooth passage of the food in the digestive tract and easy bowel action. Regular use of fruits prevents and cures constipation.

Tonic Action

Fruits, as dependable sources of vitamins, exert a tonic effect in the body. Guavas, custard apples and citrus fruits, like lemons and oranges are particularly valuable sources of vitamin C. These fruits are usually eaten fresh and raw, thus making the vitamins fully available to us. Several fruits contain good amounts of carotene which gets converted to vitamin A in the body. A medium-sized mango can provide as much as 15,000 international units of vitamin A which is sufficient for full one week and this vitamin can be stored in the body. The common papaya is an excellent source of vitamin C and carotene.

Fruits are at their best when eaten in the raw and ripe state. In cooking, they lose portions of the nutrient.

Salt and corbohydrates. They are most beneficial when taken as a separate meal by themselves, preferably for breakfast in the morning.

MEDICINAL PROPERTIES OF FRUITS

Moreover certain fruits can combat specific aliment. It should, however, be remembered that in the therapeutic use of any fruit as a treatment for specific disease, nothing except that particular fruit or its juice should be taken in the system at the time of treatment. Thus when utilising lemon juice as a food remedy, the juice should be taken in the system at the time of treatment. Thus when utilising lemon juice as a food remedy, the juice should be taken at least half an hour before consuming any other food.

It has been found that fruit sugars, calcium, iron, vitamins A, B-complex and C control the gradation of heart energy. Hence, eating fruit like apple, lemon, orange and pomegranate can aid the proper functioning of the heart and keep it healthy even in old age.Fruits like apple,date and mango have direct action on the central nervous system. The phosphorus, glutamic acid and vitamins A and B complex of these fruits exert a protective and tonic effect on the nervous exhaustion, mental tension, hysteria and insomnia.

All berries being extremely rich in iron, phosphorus and sodium, are highly beneficial for blood building and nerve strengthening. The lemon can be good food remedy in case of liver ailments, indigestion and rheumatism. Watermelons are the best kidney cleansers. The water flushes through the kidneys and traces of various minerals contained in the water act as healing agents.

The soothing qualities of pineapple and pomegranates are helpful in catarrh, hay fever and other chronic nasal and bronchial ailments. The common cold may be treated with grapefruit juice. This juice helps cure the infection by activating the orange of elimination.

Fresh and fully ripe fruits like grapes, apples, bananas and figs are best suited for all brain deficiencies. They contain a superior quality of easily digestible sugar which is transformed into physical energy that refreshes the brain. The walnut is a positive remedy for weakness of the brain.

• • •

31

Use of Vegetables to Cure Different Diseases

ACIDITY/FLATULENCE

Many persons think that potato is just a minipack of carbohydrates and fats and has no medicinal value. But in the cases of acidity and flatulence, the best treatment is to eat two potatoes cooked on the red hot sand. Then add a little of rock salt, cumin-seed, black pepper powder and sprinkle half a lemon on it. Eat this dish after meals for a week.

ANAEMIA

Tomato is the ideal vegetable to cure this trouble. Tomato is very rich in iron content which is an essential ingredient for the regeneration of blood. Besides iron it is also rich in copper content which adds haemoglobin to make blood healthy and thick red. But it is more effective when eaten raw and its juice should be sucked in. Only its seeds are not as good and may be removed.

ASTHMA

Put a layer of wet-flour (thin dough) over a freshly cut bottlegourd. Wrap it round a clean cloth and bury it in the hot sand for about half an hour. Then take it out, remove the flour layer and squeeze the bottlegourd to extract its juice. Make the patient drink this juice for 40 days for total recovery.

BLACKSPOTS

Many persons are not aware that raw tomato is a very effective stain-remover. The acidic content of tomato has the quality of removing the black spot without causing burn of the skin. The best way to do it is to apply a piece of a tomato on the spot. It is better to do so before you retire for the day. You must repeat doing so for about a week for getting the result. Soon you would find your skin acquiring its normal colour.

BLEEDING PILES

The roots of 'Chaulai ka sag' is very effective to cure this trouble. Still in the countryside this treatment is resorted to. Take about four handful of this root and grind it. Then strain it through a fine cloth. Make its karha about 3/4th of a cup. Then take 1/4th of the cup of this portion and five gms. of rasaut. Add half a gram of Nagkesar with it. Make a big wet tablet of this combination and swallow it with the remaining juice (Karha) of the Chaulai root. You must swallow this tablet immediately as it is very bitter. Continue the treatment till get rid of this trouble.

BLEEDING TEETH

After defecation and brushing your teeth in the morning, eat a fresh turnip raw, repeatedly cutting it by your teeth. This treatment will not only keep your teeth shining and firm, it will also help you get your digestives system working well.

Alternatively, wash your teeth with the water to which a little of juice of spinach has been added. Since this water is rich in chlorophyll, it helps in keeping your teeth firm and clean. Drinking tomato juice will also help.

BURNING IN SOLES

Cut the pieces of a big bottlegourd (lauki). They must be as big as to help you hold them properly. Now you lie down on your bed and ask your wife or servant to rub the pieces of the bottlegourd over your sole. Make them rub it at least for half on hour. Then you can have bath with cold water. Repeat the process for about 10 to 15 times in a month and you shall be totally cured of this trouble. If the pieces of the bottlegourd are kept inside the fridge before rubbing them, it would be still better.

BOILS & PUSTULES

These are mainly caused because of the impurity in blood. Treat them in the following way :

(i) Ask the patient to drink juice of red Bathua for three days. Make sure that he takes enough of this Bathua to have at least 30 gms. of this juice thrice every day. This will subside the extra heat accumulated in the body and consequently these boils and pustules will also disappear.

(ii) Chaulai ka Sag is also very effective to cure this trouble.

CONSTIPATION

Drinking tomato juice, having lots of Palak and Bathua in the food and having very light food are the tried and tested formula to cure constipation. Palak and Bathua are rich in iron content and their combined effect is also very lethal for the worms inside the stomach. Hence this combination not only galvanises your bowels faster but also cleans the germs inside. Besides, this dish will have another advantages. All the problems connected with the lack of generation of blood shall automatically be taken care of. Eating raw tomatoes will also help.

Diabetes

Ask the patient to eat turnip vegetable as much as he wants. Even during the off season, you can get turnip by drying it in the sun during the season and using it after boiling in water when it is not available. Another useful vegetable is tomato. Feed the patient on it but make sure that you remove the seeds in it. It is better to give the patient soup of tomatoes. If tomato juice could be added in Karela juice, this is the ideal preparation for treating this trouble.

Dyspepsia

Sucking a piece of pickle in which fenugreek has been added liberally will immediately restore your liking for food. Alternatively have red, well-ripe tomatoes raw after sprinkling a little of rock salt, black pepper and cumin seeds. Eat as much tomato as you want, but make sure that you eat more its pulp and less its seeds. If you suck a piece of tomato, it shall prove more effective. Having fresh radish with black salt and lemon-juice sprinkled on it will bring speedier relief.

Dry Skin

Drink 20 gms. of tomato juice every morning and evening. If it be winter season, add a little of lukewarm water to it. Externally, extract about 10 gms. of tomato juice and add double of coconut oil. Make their homogeneous mixture and massage your whole body with it at least half an hour before you go to take your bath. In less than a fortnight your skin will be as velvety as you desire and glowing too.

Ear-Troubles

For any ear trouble, pain or emergence of unusual sounds, treat the trouble in the following way. Add about a small bottle of Amritdhara in double of the quantity of pure mustard oil.

For any pain, just put in a few drops of this oil and plug the ear hole with a cotton, soon you will feel relief.

EMACIATED BODY

Those persons who read poronographic magazines and seek dirty company generally suffer from this problem. In fact their power of retention of their semen becomes so less that they discharge ecen at the slightest sexual reference. And since the basic fluid of the body gets weak, the whole body becomes weak. Such persons must shun such company and take lots of tomato juice. Also having spinach-seeds powder with milk early in the morning will cure this trouble.

FIRE-BURNS

(i) Mesh a raw potato and apply it on the burnt portion. The burning sensation will subside in a few moments. This is the famous fire-burns treatment.

(ii) Mesh a Parval and boil in water to get its thick Karha. When it is lukewarm drench a piece of cloth into it. Don't wring the cloth and spread it over the burnt portion. In a couple of hours the pain and burning will subside.

GOUT

The time-tested and the safest treatment for this is having tomato and Bathua mixed juice every morning and evening. Despite the combination been essentially heat giving, it cures the trouble in a couple of months. For this arrange half a kilo of Bathua, extract its juice—about 15 gms. and give it to the patient. If the patient wants he can eat tomato slices having black pepper and rock salt sprinkled over it. Also the residual part of the Bathua, whose juice has been extracted may be mixed in flour and chapatis be made of it for still quicker relief.

GASTRIC TROUBLES

Although there are numerable remedies for it. Yet the best one is the following which cures the trouble speedily and cheaply. Prepare the vegetable of brinjal and mix it with garlic and asafoetida. Eat this vegetable a little every time like you eat chutney. This will release the exam gas and activate your bowels better.

Alternatively, suck ginger juice and lemon juice having a little of rock salt sprinkled over it, after every meal.

HEART-BURNING

The burning is not exactly in the heart but over heart which is caused by indigestion. Since the pain occurs at a delicate portion, normal treatment for indigestion is not very effective. The best treatment is to mesh a raw potato and extract its juice. Make the patient drink its juice at least twice a day. Just two spoonful of juice will do. But make sure that you add no spice to the juice, even salt. Or else the trouble. If the patient can eat raw potato, it would also help.

HEART- PALPITATION

Heart-palpitation could be caused by many reasons. Nervousness, some traumatic news or the same can start it. Whenever you feel it, just have a glass of cold water, following by the juice of red Bathua. The cooling effect of the red Bathua will help considerably.

HAIR-LOSS

Those consume cabbage in large quantity rarely have this problem. In fact the sulphur content available in cabbage prevents the weakness of hair. Having brinjal will help as Iodine is also essential for the firm growth of the hair.

INSOMNIA

Vegetables, especially brinjal help cure this trouble. Make the bhurta of brinjal and mix it with white onion. First lightly roast the white onion pieces and then mix them with the brinjal or Baingun Bhurta. Eat it with chapatis as much as you want. It is better if you take this special vegetable during the night. This combination would induce sleep.

ITCHING

Even after rubbing your body clean and taking bath, you have this feeling of itching, then you must deem it to be caused by the impurity of blood. In such cases have Bathua juice twice or thrice a day. (about 10 gms.) mixed with the juice of tomato (5 gms.) only. This combination will not only cure the impurities in the blood, but shall also help in keeping your blood red and free of any infection. Have this juice twice daily for a week and the problem will be cured.

INDIGESTION

Indigestion is a common trouble caused by of taking food, at odd hours. People have a tendency of hardly chewing the eaten food—they gobble it down. That is why it is said in the Ayurvedic books that one must drink one's food (i.e., chew it as much as to make it almost liquid) and eat one's drink (i.e., drink so slowly as though you are chewing it.) If you take this precaution, eat food timely and drink a lot of water, you might not have this trouble. Eating Chaulai Ka Sag and tomato will also help.

JAUNDICE

Grind one full bittergourd and mix its juice in water. Ask the patient to drink it early in the morning. Although this would taste like bitter poison yet, it would set right the liver disorder soon. Drinking sugarcane juice and having radish with your food will also help.

Alternatively, burn about 2 kgs. of Bathua after drying it in the shades, as much as to make its ash in a clean utensil. Add seven to eight times more water to it and stir it thrice a day with your hand. After 48 hours, put it on the slow fire. When the water is vaporised, whatever remain there is the alkaline portion of Bathua. Fill in a bottle and given to the patient its 3 gms. with whey. In a week's time the infection shall be cured.

KIDNEY-TROUBLE

For all sorts of kidney trouble, including even the stone's problem use the powder of Bathua. Take this powder with a glass of lukewarm water in winters or cold water in summers. Besides, always drink a lot of water but not during meals. If you feel burning sensation in passing urine, have the juice of Kulpha-leaves thrice a day for just a week. In case the blood also passes through urine then add a little of spinach juice with water and have it for a week.

LETHARGY

To away with lethargy and making your body energetic, cabbage is the ideal vegetable. It contains ample amount of chlorine. Chlorine is believed to be the natural cleansing agent of the body. Have lots of cabbage raw or in the form of vegetable to be energetic.

LACK OF SEXUAL URGE

This trouble leads to impotence among men and to frigidity among women. The grains of seeds of fenugreek are very useful to cure this trouble. Grind the seeds to powder form and have about one or two gms. of these with a cup of milk after lunch and dinner. This will not only restore the sexual appetite but also improve the digestive system. If you find these seeds rather bitter, you may add a little of black pepper, cumin seeds, coriander-seeds, jaiphal, aniseeds, cinnamon, small and big cardamon—in short all the spices known as garam masala–in the powdered form with fenugreek seeds and take this combined powder with milk as described above. This medicine is good for both the ladies and gents.

Migraine

Take 10 gms. of Chaulai ka Sag and 10gms. of Jatamansi. Grind it to make it semi-liquid. Now add cows's 200 gms.of milk and 100 gms. of ghee. Now allow it to boil as much as to make only fat-part (ghee) remain of the solution. Keep this viscous liquid in a bottle and put a few drops of this oil into the nostril having the pain in half of the head lower than even the pillow. If there is pain be in the entire head, put this ghee in both the nostrills. A week's treatment will cure it.

Mumps

Sometimes the area around temples becomes swollen and hard, and the whole look of the face undergoes a tremendous change. Take about 5 gms. of fenugreek seeds and even amount of barley grains. Grind them together and add a little of vinegar instead of water. Make a thin paste of the both and apply it over the mumps region. In few hours the relief will be felt.

Lisping

The juice of Kulpha is ideal to improve your speaking prowess and that too speaking clearly. Not only lisping but even the inarticulate voice would also become sharp and clear.

Menstrual-Trouble

If there be obstruction in the menstrual discharge, grind 10 gms. each of the seeds of fenugreek, soya, radish and carrots to a powder form and mix the powder evenly. Take 2 gms. of this powder with fresh water every three hours. The obstruction will be cleared.

Methi is good enough not only to clear the obstruction, it also stops if menstrual discharge continues. Boil 3 gms. fenugreek seed powder in milk and allow it to boil 5 to 7 times. When cold, strain and drink this milk. The discharge will stop.

Night Blindness

As we all know this night blindness is caused by the lack of vitamin 'A' Tomato alone can take out this deficiency. The actual place of the deposit of vitamin 'A' is just below the rind of tomato. The best way to eat tomato to cure this trouble is to eat it by cutting it with your teeth. While cutting the big pieces by your teeth, suck its juice. Then you can spit out its rind and seeds. The juice of Bathua mixed with tomato is an ideal combination to cure this trouble.

Nausea

Whenever you feel nausea, either due to some concussion in the head or even otherwise, start sucking pieces of tomato on which black pepper, rock salt and lime juice have been liberally sprinkled. If you want you can add a little of fresh mint leaves over the pieces also. In fact juice of tomato, pepper, rock salt and lime juice sprinkled over it should be administered in such cases for the quick relief.

Pain in Joints

Pain in joints is caused by the deposit of hardened phlegm over these points. Cabbage is the best vegetable remedy for it as it contains ample quantity of chlorine. Chlorine clears all these impediments caused by unwanted deposit. Have raw cabbage in the form of salad and also as vegetables. If this pain be accompanied by lack of blood then the patient should also have as much beetroot as possible. Cabbage and beetroot diet will not only cure this trouble but also make body glowing in health.

PHLEGMATIC TROUBLES

For all sort of phlegmatic troubles have the Karha (decoction) made of roots of the Chaulai Ka Sag. Although the leaves of Chaulai create cold feeling in the body but their roots surge heat wave in the body. Have this Karha every night after you retire for the day for a week. If you like you can add a little ginger juice also in the Karha. Having honey every morning and evening will also help.

RICKET

Feed the child on tomato dose, either in the form of vegetable or juice. Tomatoes have the necessary vitamin 'A' to prevent the drying of the flesh and fill the child's body. Make the child eat tomato in whatever form he wants. The more tomato he eats the better he becomes. But if the heavy dose of tomato causes a purgative effect, feed the child on half of potato. Just peel off and boil potatoes, then mesh them and add a little of salt, pepper and lime juice to make them more tasty. Alternatively, you can also make sweet halwa by mixing honey with the meshed potatoes.

SWELLING OF FINGERS

Boil a few turnips in water. Rub the boiled pieces over the swollen fingers and wash them with the water in which the turnips have been boiled. Use their residual water to soak hand or feet it. If you follow this treatment for about a week's time, your fingers will become normal. Sometimes, the swelling at the joint of finger is also caused by excessive cold. That is the symptoms of the rheumatic heart. Treat first the basic cause and then start this external treatment.

SORE / BURNING THROAT

The easiest treatment for this trouble is to make poultice of the spinach leaves. Boil the spinach leaves in water and when they become soft, remove them from fire. Now grind them a bit. Heat the paste again on fire and tie it around throat for a couple of days.

For internal treatment, the best combination is licking honey and ginger juices every morning and evening. This will not only cure the throat trouble but shall also make your voice quite musical and sweet.

SCORPION BITE

Take both the variety of Chaulai Sag, the ordinary one and the thorny one. Grind both the variety to a fine paste form and apply it over the part having the string of the scorpion. When it goes dry apply another layer. Additionally make the patient drink the juice of the roots of chaulai at three hourly interval. Chaulai is a great antidote for any kind of poison infected in the body. Continue the treatment externally and internally, and in a few hours the bite's effect will be nullified.

SPLEEN SWELLING

Swelling of the spleen gives rise to many complicated diseases. The Sag of Kulpha is very effective to cure this trouble. Normally it is available in two sizes. Choti Nonia and Bari Nonia. Extract 10 gms. juice of Bari (big) Nonia and equal amount of water in it. Then make the patient drink it twice a day. Soon the spleen will be restored to its normal size. The juice of Karela is also very effective to help cure this trouble. Extract about

2 spoonfuls of Karela juice, add even amount of water and ground mustard seeds and rock salt. Make the patient drink it for just 15 days for the total relief

SPRAIN

The easiest and most effective remedy is to roast the fenugreek leaves in mustard oil. Now spread the mixture evenly in the sprained portion. Soon the injured would get relief. Even if there be internal confusion, the Methi leaves fomentation would take its care also. As an additional safety measure, make the injured person drink a glass of milk to which a pinchful of turmeric powder has been added. This internal and external treatment will bring the desired relief in a couple of hours.

SKIN TROUBLES

If your skin is oily and shining, rubbing half a lemon on the entire body before you go to take your bath is the surest and easiest remedy. Besides keeping your body free of skin trouble, the treatment would also make your body emit a fragrant, refreshing smell. In case of the dry skin, rubbing tomato juice mixed with the coconut oil is a very effective cure. In case your skin be neither very dry nor very soft and normal, then one should use oil combination for massage during the winters and the tomato combination during the summers.

STONES

To cure this trouble one should eat those vegetables which are diuretic and alkaline in effect. The alkaline content would disintegrate the stone and diuretic effect would throw the bits out through urine. Spinach or Palak had these qualities. Give twenty five gms. of Palak-juice to the patient thrice every day for three days. For a change of taste give beetroot juice after every two doses.

Trachoma in Eyes

Rub fresh raw potato on the stone and apply the extracted little juice of potato in the eyes. Not only this treatment is effective to cure trachoma, but even cataract can be dissolved by this treatment. This treatment ought to be continued till the patient begins to see clearly and brightly. In the Northern India, people still resort to this treatment with very successful results. The whole cure might take about 2 months.

Toothache

(i) Put some seeds of Brinjal over the burning cow-dung cake. Make sure that cow-dung cake may not be raw so as to emit smoke. When the seeds will touch the burning surface, they would emit smoke. Now use some hollow pipe to suck this smoke and let it tall on the aching tooth. This is a tried and tested remedy which brings relief.

(ii) Sniff a little oil of mustard by one nostril at a time. Externally mix a little rock salt, five drops of lemon juice with a couple of drops of mustard oil and allow the saliva to ooze out.

Urine Trouble

Extract the juice of Kulfa-ka-sag (or leaves) about 5 gms. and mix with it with the juice of spinach leaves, about 10 gms. Drink the potion at least thrice a day for all sorts of urine trouble. If there by scanty discharge or painful discharge or urine with a few traces of blood, this treatment will cure all of them. Continue the treatment for a couple of days. But make sure that you drink lot of water in between the dosages.

Venereal Diseases

If there be the symptoms of gonorrhoea in men, the disease shows itself in the irritation of the urethra, scalding pain on passing urine and a viscid yellowish- white discharge; in women, it begins with a yellow vaginal discharge, pain on passing urine and very often inflammation of the glands situated close to the uvula, the patient should be given water mixed in milk and also the juice of Chaulai leaves. Prepare the Chaulai juice in the following way. Put about a handful of chaulai leaves in boiling water for and allow it to cool off. When lukewarm, strain through a fine cloth and keep this water drinking purpose. Whenever the patient feels thirsty he must take either this water or milk water solution or better take them alternately. The entire infection should clear out by means of urine and in about a fortnight's time he would get relief. Such patients must not sit on hard seat and should shun reading dirty and cheap magazine and indulging in sexual intercourse.

WEAK EYE SIGHT

The ideal treatment of the weak eye-sight would be having lots of tomatoes and cured as the weakness of the sight is caused due to lack of vitamin 'A' in the body. You can use curd and tomato combination either in the form of vegetable or as syrup. In about two parts of tomato juice, beat one part of fresh curd. If it to be salty, add a little of rocksalt, a piece or two of onion, black pepper and cumin seed. Add finely cut coriander leaves to make it more tasty. Have it in your lunch and dinner. If you want it to be sweet, then add a little of jaggery and sugar.

WEAK BRAIN

Since beetroot is full of iron, calcium and phosphorus, eating beetroot either in the form of salad or vegetable goes a long way to provide strength to the brain cells. Beetroot will also provide the necessary constituents to the body to make it more red and hence a better capacity to assimilate the absorbed oxygen. When you eat beetroot as salad, cut the soft leaves also of the beetroot.

Have this salad as much as you want and in a couple of days you would start getting the desired effect.

WHITE SPOTS ON THE BODY

For spots on the body, the freshly cut pieces of tomatoes provides quick relief. Wherever these are, just tie the pieces of tomato over them. Leave them as it is for a few hours. Still better if you tie the pieces of tomato over the affected spots when you retire for the day. In the morning you can take your normal bath without using soap. For internal treatment, have tomatoes and fresh coconut as many times as you like. These spots occur because of the lack of calcium in the body and this tomato and coconut diet will make this deficiency.

WORMS IN INTESTINES

Bathua is the ideal medicine to cure this trouble. Extract the juice of Bathua, about two or two and a half spoonful and add a little to rock-salt to it. Make the patient drink it at least thrice a day, preferably after principal meals. Additionally, make the patient eat Bathua in the vegetable form. Bathua is very effective to cure the worms. Besides, it is a very good laxative and not only the worms are killed, the laxative effect shall clean them out of the system also.

WEAK DIGESTION

Weak digestion results because of the excessive consumption of fatty, fried and rich food, that too at irregular hours. The tension of modern life also adds to this trouble. These adverse condition put extra pressure on the liver which is further aggravated by taking alcoholic drinks. And it must be remembered that there is no medicine to cure a damaged liver. So, having regulated, light diet and following strict regimen is the only way to cure the trouble. One must plan one's day's menu and strictly adhere to it.

Begin your morning by having a lukewarm water-a glassful-with half a lemon's juice squeezed into it. Then take light breakfast or porridge and germinated grams, followed by milk. In lunch have curds, grams, followed by milk. Bathua and fresh salad having cabbage, beetroot and radishes. Take just a glassful of mosambi juice in the afternoon. In dinner have tomato palak mixed juice, salad, and chapatis made of gram flour. End your day's menu by having a glassful of lukewarm milk with isabgol. In less than a week's time, you would get the desired relief.

WEAKNESS IN GENERAL

If one continues to take, tomato, cabbage, spinach, bathua, beetroots and milk, one is not likely to develop any weakness. Because these vegetable and leaves supply the necessary vitamins and mineral essential to keep body in good trim. Potato, cauliflower and tomato's combination not only gives a very tasty vegetable but it is also full of nutritional elements. For even sexual weakness, tomato is a very patent cure. Have tomato juice in the morning and follow it up by the ground seeds of spinach, to be washed down with plain milk. Not many people are aware that the seeds of spinach are a very powerful aphrosodiac. If one sticks to this diet for about a month and doesn't indulge in sexual intercourse, one would become as sturdy as an ox in every way and his body would not only be powerful, and full of life.

• • •

32

Condiments and Spices as Medicines

1. **Ajwain** stops hiccups and flatulence, and has antiseptic qualities.
2. **Dhania** has a very cooling effect in fever.
3. **Elaichi** is good for a cough, suppresses vomiting when eaten with banana, and is a good digestive aid.
4. **Garammasala** enhances the flour of food and helps in digestion.
5. **Haldi** reduces fat, purifies and circulates blood, enhances the body colour and works as best antiseptic element.
6. **Jeera** is very cooling, with a sweet taste.
7. **Javantri** is rejuvenating, improves appetite and digestion.
8. **Jaiphal** - as Javantri
9. **Kesar** - as Javantri
10. **Kalajeera** is cooling but with a strong or bitter taste.
11. **Khus Khus** is binding, helpful against diarrhoea.
12. **Laung** is helpful in cough and colds.
13. **Mirchi** is helpful in digestion, hair growth.
14. **Methi** is helpful in coughs and colds, as well as joints problems.
15. **Mari** is good for the heart, increases appetite.
16. **Rai** kills germs, removes gastric distension.

17. **Sava** suppresses hiccups, vomiting and painful wind in children.
18. **Taj** clears throat, removes thirst, improves appetite.
19. **Til** oil thickens and lengthens hair, massaged on gums firms teeth, best for body massage.
20. **Variyali** is useful in reducing fever.

Beans

When any bean is split it is called dal, e.g. chana dal, mung dal, etc. The general term for flour made from any bean is aata.

Indian Name	English Name	Comments
Channa	Chick pea	Used in excess quantity will cause wind
Chola	Black-eye bean	Cook with a good quantity of oil to reduce wind
Mung	Green garam	Most easily digested of all the beans produces the least wind
Masur	Red split dal	Cook with plenty of oil, removes fever
Rajma	Kidney bean	Very healthy bean, reduces impurity in the blood and imparts strength
Vatana	Soya bean	Heavy bean, cook with plenty of oil, very tasty
Tuver	Split yellow ochre lentil	Very healthy bean, improves skin texture
Urad	Black gram	Rejuvenating
Val	Indian baked bean	Cook with plenty of oil, weight produces Vata

TEN DO NOTS

1. DO NOT USE tinned Food
2. DO NOT USE food with preservatives
3. DO NOT USE food colouring

4. DO NOT USE artificial flavouring.
5. DO NOT USE white sugar
6. DO NOT USE white flour
7. DO NOT USE white rice
8. DO NOT USE margarine
9. DO NOT USE microwave ovens
10. DO NOT USE cold or stale food.

drs108@gmail.com
www.newkamasutra.com

• • •

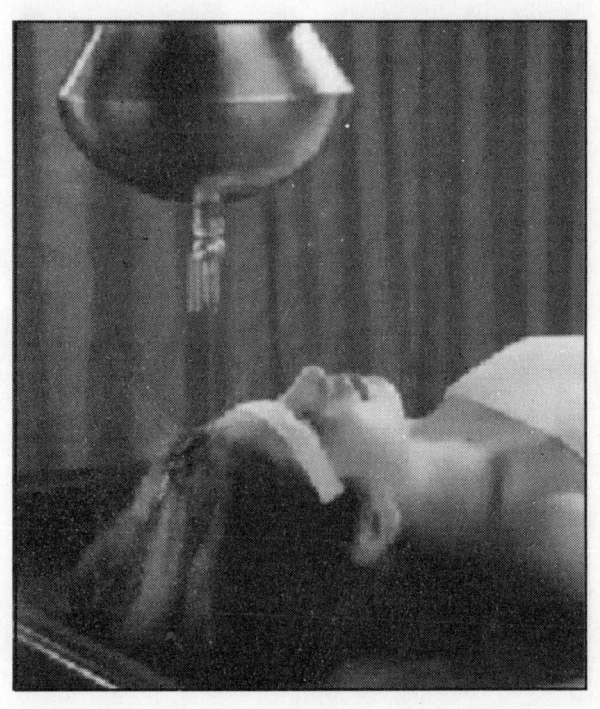

Part – V

33

Panchakarma and Other Ayurvedic Treatments

Specialized ayurvedic remedies such as panchakarma, marma chikitsa, dhara or following an ayurvedic diet, basically endeavour to restore the harmony of the tridoshas. The purpose of all ayurvedic remedies and herbal medicines is to keep the doshas or the humours in equilibrium, since an imbalance indicates a disease condition. Samsodhana (cleansing process), samsamana (palliative measures) and nidanaparivarjana (treating the causes) are the three main stages through which ayurvedic remedies usually progress.

Of these three remedial phases, samsodhana is considered a prominent process and according to ayurveda, should be administered with full care. Panchakarma is synonymous with this process. In fact, panchakarma is a group of five ayurvedic remedies, all of which are not practiced in all diseases.

Panchakarma

Ayurveda recognizes that all living and non-living things are composed of panchamahabhut or five basic elements of the entire creation. One branch of Indian philosophy—Sankhya, states that there are 24 elements in all, of which five are the foundation of the gross world: earth, water, fire, air and ether. According to ayurveda these five elements in different combinations constitute the three body types/doshas—vata (air and ether), pitta (fire) and kapha (earth and water). These two theories are the guiding factors of ayurveda as a therapeutic science.

Ayurveda advises undergoing panchakarma at the seasonal changes to both keep the metabolism strong and keep toxins from accumulating in the body as well as the mind. The process finds the way to the root cause of the problem and corrects the essential balance of mind, body, and emotions. It is considered extremely effective to go through the process of panchakarma prior to any rejuvenation treatment (rasayana/herbal medicines), for it cleanses the body, improves the digestion, the metabolic processes of the body and cleanse the thought process as well.

Basically, panchakarma is meant to make an individual most receptive to the curative process of ayurveda by removing accumulated waste in body and mind.

VAMANA (EMESIS)

It is a process of therapeutic vomiting (induced), which helps eliminate the toxic or waste matters from the stomach and thoracic cavity. Kapha dominant diseases like severe skin diseases (psoriasis, urticaria); bronchial asthma, mental disorders etc. are selected for this treatment procedure. This process is not suggested for expecting mothers. Normally eight bouts of emesis are followed. The vomiting is stopped when yellow coloration is seen. Then, dhoomapana—inhalation of medicated fumes—is done through a special process. Finally, certain rules have to be followed called paschatkarma that basically implies strict diet regimen.

The entire treatment takes 15 days, and requires good attention as well as skilled assistance.

VIRECHANA (PURGATION)

This eliminates the toxic or waste matters from the intestine. It also cures pitta or pitta-dominated diseases. Poorvakarma or initial process of cleansing like vamana is suggested here. About 20 purges may be seen in this process depending on the patient's health. A mild form of virechana without the poorvakarma, is an integral part of ayurvedic therapy. It is also used for prevention of diseases.

VASTI (ENEMA)

The process of vasti or therapeutic enema is resorted to eliminate toxins from colon, and strengthens the tissues. Two kinds of vastis are followed in ayurveda. Snehavasti is the vasti where medicated oils are used. This is not advised in patients suffering from diabetes, anaemia, diarrhoea, and obesity. Poorvakarma is required here.

For kashaya vasti, honey, rock salt, sneham (oils), paste of medicines are required and mixed one by one in the above order. This concoction is taken in an empty stomach. After the process the patient is allowed to take a bath.

Diseases like hemiplegia, and disease due to vata are treated by this process. Medicines are selected as per disease and stage.

NASYA (NASAL APPLICATION OF HERBAL MEDICINES)

Nasya is instillation of medicine through nose. It is an important procedure of ayurveda for the treatment of sirorogas or diseases affecting head area. Nasya helps cleanse the head and sinuses. The process is contraindicated in various psychological diseases, asthma and cough. Here, the patient is to inhale lightly warmed oil. Warmed oil is massaged in the patient's neck, shoulder, palm, face and sole before and after the process of nasya. Different timings are indicated for different dosha types. Morning time is prescribed for kapha diseases, noon in pitta diseases and evening in vata diseases.

Raktamoksha (Blood-Letting)

Susruta gave stress to Raktamoksha (blood-letting) as one of the panchakarma, taking two of the vastis as a single karma. The process of letting out the vitiated blood is termed raktamoksha. In this procedure localized impurity or poison from the blood is removed through various methods. Often leech is used to suck out the impure blood from the affected area. Blood-letting is also done to eliminate toxins from the blood stream causing various chronic skin disorders like urticaria, eczema, scabies and leucoderma etc. The method was also effectively used to cure enlarged liver and spleen.

There are steps to be followed before doing panchakarma called poorvakarma. One is snehana or oleation where medicated oils are applied internally and externally. Another process called swedana or sudation is actually classified into four types to induce sweating. The purpose of poorvakarma is to liquefy and guide the provoked doshas to the mainstream to facilitate the sodhana or cleansing.

Diet

Following a strict ayurvedic diet also forms part of the ayurvedic treatment method. Ayurveda emphasizes that the diet we take has a close influence on our mind and body. According to ayurveda, the mind has three possible states (tri-gunas) that are related to the three states of our physical constitution or the three-dosha types. Sattva, or peaceful equilibrium, rajas, or excessive activity and tamas, or inertia—the three tendencies or gunas of mind influence the imbalances in the three doshas. Specific dietary adjustments serves to maintain the balance of specific doshas and thus entail perfect health. Appropriate diet can be used to remove or neutralize toxins in the body also.

Ayurveda suggests eating food until one's appetite is satisfied. When ill, one should eat only light food, and then normal food in small quantities, until half the appetite is fulfilled. One important rule in ayurveda is never to combine contradictory foods in terms of their qualities. Some of the commonly followed rules on food habits according to ayurveda are as below:

- Keeping high-protein or high-fat food items in separate meals from lighter foods such as starches and vegetables.
- Not mixing milk with yogurt.
- Not eating cooked foods and raw foods at the same meal since they require different types of digestion.
- Avoiding drinking milk while eating radishes, tomatoes, meat, fish, eggs, citrus fruits.
- Eating fresh fruit separately from other meals (except the cooked fruits).
- Some specific vegetables and grains are forbidden in some specific days of a month. Diet is to be compatible with changing seasons.

YOGA

Practice of yoga is an integral method in ayurveda, which is applied to keep both the body and mind healthy and relaxed. It is recommended for cure as well as for prevention of various ailments. Different yogasanas are prescribed for different dosha based ailments. The lifestyle regimens mentioned in yoga are integral to ayurvedic treatment. Meditation is often recommended to maintain balance or peace in the thinking process. Meditation removes any disturbances in the balance of the three mental states of sattva, rajas and tamas.

Gems

Recommendation of gems to avoid any imminent problem is associated with Jyotish Shastra (astrology). Ayurveda applies Jyotish Shastra (astrology) to ascertain the imminent diseases an individual is going to suffer as well as to ascertain what type of gems would be beneficial for him. Ayurveda prescribes nine precious gemstones to be used externally and internally as well. Apart from recommending wearing gems, the rasayana branch of ayurveda, also, recommends calxes of various gemstones (bhasma) as internal medicine.

Marma Chikitsa (Vital Points)

Marma Chikitsa is a significant aspect of the ayurvedic treatment. Marmas are specific points on the body where the application of pressure or insertion of needles (bhedana) induces the flow of vital energy (prana) along a complex system of subtle channels called (nadis). Basing on the knowledge enumerated in Dhanur Veda (deals in martial art), ayurveda recognizes about 350 therapeutic marma points and over 100 lethal marma points within our body. The injury to some of these lethal marma points can lead to instant death. Massage is widely applied in the treatment of marmas.

Dhara (Oil)

Oil is an integral ingredient in ayurvedic treatment. Sesame oil and ghee (Butter oil) is commonly used. Oil can be administered internally as nasal-drops (nasya) or can be used for mouth gurgling. The external oiling is in the form of a massage. Specific oils are used for individuals having specific dosha types of vata, pitta and kapha.

Kaya Kalpa

Kaya kalpa literally means renewal of the body. This is a unique method of treating both the gross and the subtle body to prolong the youthfulness and vigour in younger people, and revive the vitality in old. The treatment method of kaya kalpa is considered to be the culmination of ayurvedic knowledge as a complete medical science. The two significant branches of ayurveda—kayachikitsa and rasayana deal with this method.

• • •

34

Five Elements Theory
Air, Earth, Water, Fire, Ether

According to the Five Elements Theory, the human being is a small model of the universe. What exists in the human body exists in altered form in the universal body. Ayurveda believes that everything is made up of five elements, or building blocks: earth, water, fire, air, and ether. Their properties are important in understanding balances and imbalances in the human body.

Earth is representative of the solid state of matter; it manifests stability, fixity and rigidity. We see around us rocks and soil standing against the wearing forces of water and wind. Our body also manifests this earth/solid state structure: bones, cells and tissue are physical structures through which our blood courses and oxygen is transported. Earth is considered a stable substance.

Water characterizes change. In the outer world we see water moving through its cycles of evaporation/clouds/condensation/rain, we see it moving around solid matter such as rocks and mountains, and we see it eventually wearing away solid, immovable matter as it flows from the mountains to the sea. We see rivers carrying dissolved soil and nutrients, carrying economic trade and exchange of information and culture, we see the earth's bodies of water nurturing life everywhere. Our blood, lymph, and other fluids move between our cells and through our vessels, bringing energy, carrying away wastes, regulating temperature, bringing disease fighters, and carrying hormonal information from one area to another. Water is considered a substance without stability.

Fire is the power to transform solids to liquids, to gas, and back again. The heat of the sun melts ice into water that becomes vapour under its influence. Fire provides power to the water and weather cycles of nature. The sun's energy is the initiator of all energy cycles on earth- including all food chains. Within our bodies it is fire (energy) that binds the atoms of our molecules together; that converts food to fat (stored energy) and muscle' that turns (burns) food into energy; that creates the impulses of nervous reactions, our feelings and even our thought processes. Fire is considered form without substance.

Air is the gaseous form of matter which is mobile and dynamic. We do not see the air that blows through the tree's leaves, but we feel it. We know how material it can be - how it can respond to energy, absorb it, and give it off- when we watch or experience a hurricane, typhoon or tornado. We feel air as it courses down our throats and into our lungs- cut that off for more than a few minutes and we know with our whole being how fundamental air is to life. Within the body, air (oxygen) is the basis for all energy transfer reactions - oxidation. Clean and pure, it is a key element required for fire to burn. Air is existence without form.

Ether is the space in which everything happens. Like outer space with millions of miles between celestial bodies, or the inner space of our bodies where our very atoms are only .00001 charged particle and .99999 emptiness. Space, the distance between things- which helps to define one thing from another. Ether is only the distances which separate matter.

The Three Doshas

In Ayurvedic philosophy, the five elements combine in parts to form three dynamic forces (interactions) called doshas. Dosha means "that which changes" because doshas are constantly moving in dynamic balance, one with the others. Doshas are primary life forces or biological humours. They are only found in life forms (similar to the concepts of organic chemistry), and their dynamism is what makes life happen.

The Five Elements Combine to Create the Three Doshas (Forces)

Vata (va-ta) is a force conceptually made up of the elements ether and air. The proportions of ether and air determine how active Vata is. The amount of ether (space) affects the ability of air to gain momentum, as expressed in Vata. In the body, Vata is movement (a dynamism of the combination between ether and air), and manifests itself in living things as the movement of nerve impulses, air, blood, food, waste and thoughts.

Vata has seven characteristics, which are : cold, light, irregular, mobile, rarefied, dry, and rough. These qualities characterize their effect on the body. Too much Vata force can cause nerve irritation, high blood pressure, gas and confusion.

Too little Vata, we have nerve loss, congestion, constipation and thoughtlessness.

Pitta (pit-ta) is a force conceptually created by the dynamic interplay of water and fire. These two seemingly opposed forces represent transformation. They cannot change into each other, but they modulate each other and are vitally necessary to each other in the life processes.

In our bodies Pitta is manifested by the quality of transformation. Pitta is the enzymes which digest our food and the hormones which regulate our metabolism. In our mind, the Pitta force is the transformation of chemical/electrical impulses into understood thoughts. Too much Pitta can cause ulcers, hormonal imbalance, irritated skin (acne), and consuming emotions (anger). Too little Pitta and we have indigestion, inability to understand and sluggish metabolism.

The Pitta force is described according to eight characteristics which affect the body: hot, light, fluid, subtle, sharp, malodorous, soft and clear.

Kapha (ka-fa) is the conceptual equilibrium of water and earth. Kapha is structure and lubrication-it draws on the conceptual characteristics of the elements of earth and water. At one level, Kapha is the cells which make up our organs and the fluids which nourish and protect them.

In the Ayurvedic organization of cause and effect, too much Kapha force causes mucous buildup in the sinus and nasal passages, the lungs and colon. In the mind it creates rigidity, a fixation of thought, inflexibility. Not enough Kapha force causes the body to experience a dry respiratory tract, burning stomach (due to lack of mucous, which gives protection from excess stomach acids), and inability to concentrate. Kapha force is expressed according to the following qualities: oily, cold, heavy, stable, dense and smooth.

CHANGING FORCES

These three dynamic forces are constantly changing and balancing each other in all living things. They make life happen. In a plant, Vata is concentrated in the flowers and leaves (which reach farthest out into space and air), Kapha is concentrated in the rots (where water is stored in the embrace of earth), and Pitta is found in the plants' essential oils, resins and sap (especially in spices which stimulate digestion.) Different plants have different concentrations of V-P-K (Vata, Pitta, Kapha). We can use different foods, plants, and specific plant parts to alter our body's proportion of V-P-K. Eating root vegetables, milk products, or sedating herbs like valerian, increases our Kapha. Drinking herbal flowers like jasmine, or eating dry grains, increases our Vata forces. Eating hot, spicy foods like cayenne, or concentrated protein like bee pollen, increases our Pitta tendencies.

CLIMATIC INFLUENCES

The climates we live in and the change of seasons also add or subtracts from our V-P-K balance. Hot summers or hot climates increase our Pitta. Dry climates or cold autmn winds increases Vata. Wet winters and damp climates add to Kapha.

LIFE STAGES

The stage of life we are in also affects V-P-K balance. The increase in the substance of the body which occurs during childhood growth means that Kapha forces are dominant during this cycle of life. The hormone changes which transform us into adults indicate that our early and middle years are under Pitta influence. As we age, we can shrink and dry out, indicating and increase of Vata forces.

AYURVEDIC CYCLES OF THE DAY

As told by Jean - Pierre LeBlanc (of Aroma Joy, B.C., Canada)

Kapha 1 Cycle 6:00 a.m. - 10:00a.m.

All movements slow down. If you sleep past 6:00 a.m. it's harder to get up and you feel groggy. Food eaten now will not digest as well and should be light.

PITTA 1 CYCLE 10:00 A.M.- 2:00 P.M.

Your metabolism gears up to its highest at 12:00 noon. This is the best time to eat your largest or most concentrated meal and take vitamins for greater absorption.

VATA 1 CYCLE 2:00 P.M.-6:00 P.M.

A time of increased movement and activity. Your evening meals should be lighter than lunch. Mental activity and conversation should be lively.

KAPHA II CYCLE 6:00 P.M.-10:00 P.M.

The energy slows down for bed and rest. Sleep will come easily and quickly. If you don't go to sleep by 10:00 p.m. you toss and turn, especially if you eat late.

PITTA II CYCLE 10:00 P.M.- 2:00 A.M.

Time of active, colourful dreams and deep sleep. If you happen to stay up, your metabolism may get geared up for a late night snack and activities, which you will regret the next day.

Vata II Cycle 2:00 a.m. - 6:00 a.m.

Corresponds to the ascending universal currents which are used by meditators to achieve high spiritual states. If you wake up at 4:00 or 5:00 a.m. and do spiritual exercise it will stay with you all day long as focused energy. If you sleep past 6:00 a.m., you fall into lethargic Kapha time.

• • •

Part – VI

35

Drugs and Herbs of Ayurveda used in Treatment of Cancer

There are many drugs for the treatment of Cancer. Though, it is not recommended to treat yourself for such a fatal disease, but for your knowledge, some medicines are elaborated for specific carcinoma's. Please consult some learned ayurvedic physician for further information.

1. **Drugs and herbs of Ayurveda used according to specific system location.**

   (a) **Brain Cancers - Ayurvedic Herbs**
   –Mandukaparni (Bacopa monerea)
   –Kastoori Bhairave Rasa with combination of divya herbs.

   (b) **Oropharyngeal Cancers - Ayurvedic Herbs**
   –Kasamarda (cassia oxidentalis)
   –Mahalaxmi vilas Rasa

   (c) **Lung Cancers - Ayurvedic Herbs**
   –Pippali (Piper longum)
   –Hirak Rasayan

   (d) **Stomach Cancers - Ayurvedic Herbs**
   –Shatavari (Asparagus resimosus)
   –Amlaki (Philanthus amblica)
   –Banga Bhasma
   –Aloe-Vera

- Amaltas (Casia fistula)
- Bhoy-Amli (Philanthus nurare)
- Sarphunkha (Tephrosia purpua)

(e) **Intestinal Cancers - Ayurvedic Herbs**
- Shigru (Moringa Olifera)
- Panchamrut purpti

(f) **Female Genital Cancers - Ayurvedic Herbs**
- Ashoka (Seraka Ashoka)
- Vaikranta Bhasma

(g) **Main Genital Cancers - Ayurvedic Herbs**
- Triphala (Three myrobelans)
- Makardhvaja

(h) **Liver Cancers - Ayurvedic Herbs**
- Bhumvamalaki
- Arogyavardhini

(i) **Blood Cancer - Ayurvedic Herbs**
- Anantmula (Hermidesmus indicus)
- Suvarna Vasant Malti Rasa

(j) **Bone Cancer - Ayurvedic Herbs**
- Aabha Gugglu
- Madhu Malini Vasant Rasa

(k) **Breast Cancer - Ayurvedic Herbs**
- Gojivha
- Chinchabhallataka

(l) **Skin Cancer - Ayurvedic Herbs**
- Mangishtha (Rubia cordifolia)
- Samira Panaga Rasa
- Kaishore Gugglu
- Gandhak Rasayan

2. **Drugs of Ayurveda according to to the general condition of the patient**
- Sutashekhar rasa
- Punarnava Mandura

- Aarogya Vardhini
- Avipattikar Churna
- Kamadhugdha Rasa
- Swarna Gairika
- Laghu Vasant Malti
- Hirak Bhasma

3. **Drugs of Ayurveda according to the Agni of the patient**
   - Drakshasava
   - Swarna Makshika Bhasma
   - Shivakshara Pachan Churna
   - Chitrakadi Vati
   - Triphala Churna
   - Panchskhar Churna

4. **Drugs of Ayurveda used in all cancers**
   - Kanchnara Gugglu
   - Kaishore Gugglu
   - Bhallatak Phalmajja Churna
   - Triphala Gugglu
   - Tribang Bhasma
   - Shilajatu Vati
   - Aabha Gugglu
   - Laksha Gugglu

5. **Drugs of Ayurveda according to Nadi**
   - Vishtinduka for Vatta Nadi
   - Katuki for Pitta Nadi
   - Bhallatak for kapha Nadi
   - Combination of above for dvidosha Nadi
   - All three for Tridosh Nadi

6. **Decoctions of Ayurveda for purification of body cells prescribed to all patients. One, two or more from the following**
   - Varunadi Kwath
   - Panchvalkal Kwath
   - Manjishathadki Kwath
   - Dashmula Kwath
   - Varunadi Kwath
   - Kanchnar Kwath

7. **Drugs of Ayurveda for Symptomatic relief**
   - All Gugglu preparations for pain relief, and tumor reducing.
   - Gandhak Rasayan for infections
   - Bilva, Mayurpichha, Tankan, sphatika for loose motions and vomiting
   - Shigru, Chitrakadivati for pain in the abdomen
   - Rohitaka, Shamaka yoga for pain in pancreas and renal colic.
   - Shirashooladivajra rasa, for headaches
   - Beejapuraka and trikatu in jaundice
   - Vasa+Goat milk in bleeding
   - Aabha+Madhumandura in bone pain

8. **DARF methodology to reduce the side effects of chemotherapy**
   Some of the most common side effects of chemotherapy
   - Mucositis-in the form of mouth ulcers, vomiting, loose motions etc.
   - Phlebities-in the form of skin discolouration with veins paining

- Leukopenia-in the form of low w.b.c. counts with increased chances of infection
- Hair loss

Thearapies three days prior to chemotherapy

- Sadhya Snehan-One teaspoon cow ghee+one teaspoon salt, mixed and consumed at morning, empty stomach with hot water.
- Manjishthadi Kwath and Kanchnar Gugglu. During chemotherapy, coriander leaves juice freshly prepared about 20 to 30 gms, twice a day.

Treatment during Radiotherapy

- Sadhya snehan + Matra basti for three days
- A piece of tamarind to be kept in mouth during R.T. is advised in mouth and throat cancers.
- A vaginal tampon of Erand oil is applied daily in vaginal cervical and rectal cancers
- Amrudu virechan Mild laxative is always advised during R.T. except in vaginal and cervical cancers
- Symptomatic treatment as per the situation is offered.

Note: Please consult your physician for further information. Avoid self trial.

• • •

Other Books on Health

1. Ayurveda for All (New) — 150/-
2. A Guide to Migraine, Arthritis, Cervical Spondylosis and Backache (New) — 125/-
3. Body and Beauty Care (New) — 125/-
4. Yoga for All (New) — 250/-
5. Child Care and Nutrition (New) — 95/-
6. Naturopathy Modern Way of Life (New) — 125/-
7. A Guide to Your Pregnancy (New) — 150/-
8. First Aid (How to Handle an Accident) — 125/-
9. Acupressure in Daily Life — 125/-
10. Complete Book of Yoga — 150/-
11. Look Younger at any Age — 125/-
12. HIV/AIDS-Transmission, Prevention — 110/-
13. Diabetics and Diet — 110/-
14. Increase your Height & Loose your Weight — 125/-
15. Make Fitness A Way of Life — 195/-
16. Common Problems of Children — 150/-
17. Handbook of Nutrition and Dietetics — 250/-
18. A Guide to Massage Therapy — 125/-
19. A Guide to Family Medicine — 150/-
20. A Guide to Digestive Disorders — 125/-
21. Complete Book of Child Care — 150/-
22. A Guide to Homoeopathy — 125/-
23. Life Begins at 40 — 125/-
24. Alternative Therapies — 125/-

25. How to Overcome Stress	110/-
26. Yoga Therapy	225/-
27. Obesity	125/-
28. Self Motivation	125/-
29. Yoga for Health and Relaxation	95/-
30. Women Disorders and Pregnancy	110/-
31. A Guide to Body Pains	95/-
32. Sex Education	95/-
33. Common Diseases and Cure	95/-
34. Pranayama for Better Life	95/-
35. Herbal Home Remedies	95/-
36. A Guide to Beauty and Skin Care	95/-
37. A Guide to Heart Care	95/-
38. A Guide to High Blood Pressure	90/-
39. Cancer: Causes and Prevention	95/-
40. Nature Cure for Common Diseases	95/-
41. Good Health Through Food and Regimen	90/-
42. A Guide to Allergies	125/-
43. A Guide to Aging	95/-
44. Ayurveda for Health & Beauty	95/-

4263/3, Ansari Road,
Darya Ganj, New Delhi-110 002
Ph. : 32903912, 23280047, 9811594448
E-mail: lotus_press@sify.com
www.lotuspress.co.in